Conjugal Union

What Marriage Is and Why It Matters

PATRICK LEE
Franciscan University of Steubenville

ROBERT P. GEORGE
Princeton University

D0869460

CAMBRIDGE
UNIVERSITY PRESS

CAMBRIDGE
UNIVERSITY PRESS

32 Avenue of the Americas, New York, NY 10013-2473, USA

Cambridge University Press is part of the University of Cambridge.

It furthers the University's mission by disseminating knowledge in the pursuit of education, learning, and research at the highest international levels of excellence.

www.cambridge.org
Information on this title: www.cambridge.org/9781107670556

© Patrick Lee and Robert P. George 2014

First published 2014

Printed in the United States of America

A catalog record for this publication is available from the British Library.

Library of Congress Cataloging in Publication Data
Lee, Patrick, 1952–
Conjugal union : what marriage is and why it matters / Patrick Lee, Franciscan University of Steubenville Robert P. George, Princeton University.
    pages cm
Includes bibliographical references and index.
ISBN 978-1-107-05992-4 (hardback) – ISBN 978-1-107-67055-6 (paperback)
1. Marriage.   I. George, Robert P.   II. Title.
HQ519.L4395   2014
306.81–dc23   2014007207

ISBN 978-1-107-05992-4 Hardback
ISBN 978-1-107-67055-6 Paperback

Contents

Acknowledgments

For invaluable assistance and support for this book, we wish to thank George Creel and the National Catholic Community Foundation, Jamie McAleer, John McAleer, Luis Tellez and the Witherspoon Institute, Ryan Anderson, Joseph Boyle, Gerard Bradley, Christian Brugger, John Finnis, Sherif Girgis, Mary Ann Glendon, Germain Grisez, John Haldane, Daniel Mark, William E. May, Alejandro Miranda, Melissa Moschella, Peter Ryan, S.J., and Christopher Tollefsen.

Introduction

During a recent daytime television talk show, a young woman was informed that her husband had offered her best friend five hundred dollars to have sex with him. Needless to say, the young woman (the wife) became very angry, and she (along with the talk show host and most of the audience present) viewed this act as an egregious betrayal. During the heated argument that ensued, it emerged that the unfortunate wife would have been just as angry if her husband had offered a much smaller sum; and, by contrast, she would have been much *less* angry if he had offered even a larger sum in return for something other than sex. What particularly hurt her (and angered the host and the live audience) was, not the money, but the fact that her husband was seeking sex from her friend. The husband objected that if he had had sex with his wife's friend, it would not have been an expression of love and would not have detracted from what *they* had, which was very special. However, neither the young lady nor the audience seemed impressed by this logic. It was clear that, according to the wife, the in-studio audience, and the talk show host, the young man's sexual acts, both real and hoped for, could not be described (as he sought to describe them) as meaningless.

Who was right, the young woman or the young man? Is there something special about sexual acts, or do they have meaning only if we choose to impose it on them? Why should a wife care if her husband engages in "meaningless" sex with her best friend? What makes sexual acts so different – at least in our perception – from other types of activities? Someone might say that the young man in question had promised to have sex only with his wife, and that she felt betrayed only because he broke that promise. But of course, breaking a promise about some other issue would not have been so serious a matter. Moreover, this pushes the question back: why are people even inclined to promise to have sex only with their wives or husbands to begin with? The fact that at least many people are inclined to do so suggests that there is *something* special about sex. But what is it? What makes sex so much more meaningful (in most cases, anyway) than playing tennis together, sharing an interest in nineteenth-century English literature (or contemporary Hollywood gossip), or forming a business partnership?

And yet, since the 1960s, the idea that sex can be just a fun thing to do, without serious meaning or consequences, has gained significant ground in our culture. The central idea of the sexual revolution was that young men and (especially) women should shake themselves free of the "benighted" and "repressive" idea that sexual acts should be reserved for marriage and embrace a "liberated" view of sex as a form of recreation bound only by the principle of "consent." In certain circles, young women and men, and increasingly, girls and boys, are *expected* to think and behave according to this idea. The view that sex lacks any inherent meaning is conveyed in countless television shows – sitcoms, dramas, and talk shows – in movies, and in sex education (and "health") classes.

Of course, this shift in attitudes toward sex was precipitated, at least in part, by the introduction of the anovulent birth control pill in the early 1960s. It was then generally thought that unmarried men and women could now have sex without fear of the bad consequences that had held them (especially women) back before. In addition, the conviction that sex should be reserved for marriage was viewed as part of Victorian repression. The revolution was supposed to liberate women (and men, if they needed such liberation) so they could now have sex without worrying about physical and emotional consequences – pregnancy, guilt, and emotional entanglements. This idea has persisted: on television or in the movies, one only occasionally sees anyone become pregnant, discover that he or she has an incurable sexually transmitted disease, or experience emotional difficulties resulting from what were meant to be casual sexual encounters.

And yet the promise of consequence-free sex has for many men and women turned out to be illusory. For one thing, contraceptives have a significant failure rate. Even the pill has a significant user rate of failure – as is made clear when it is argued that abortion must be available as a backup for contraceptives.[1] Then, too, abortion is never merely a minor inconvenience – it often has significant negative effects on the emotional well-being of women who undergo the procedure, and always on the unborn human beings whose lives are extinguished.

Moreover, the increase in nonmarital sexual activity has led to a dramatic increase in sexually transmitted infections and diseases – some of which were exceedingly rare or even unknown before the 1970s and 1980s.

Finally, many women commenting on the shift in sexual attitudes and behaviors in the last few decades have explained that sexual acts that were supposed to be casual or recreational often turn out not to be so emotionally meaningless for one of the parties. According to these writers, after such sexual activity, women frequently experience a feeling of being used or of hollowness. As Canadian journalist and author Danielle Crittenden explains:

Indeed, in all the promises made to us about our ability to achieve freedom and independence as women, the promise of sexual emancipation may have been the most illusory. Yes, we can do "anything a man does" (except maybe in terms of bench pressing). And yet, all the sexual bravado a young woman may possess evaporates the first time a man she truly cares for makes it clear that he has no further use for her after his own body has been satisfied. No amount of feminist posturing, no amount of reassurances that she doesn't need a guy like that anyway, can protect her from the pain and humiliation of those awful moments

---

[1] See Planned Parenthood of Southeastern Pennsylvania v. Casey, 505 U.S. 833, 856 (1992).

after he's gone, when she's alone – and feeling not sexually empowered, but discarded . . . This "used" feeling among women is one that has not gone away after 30 years of experimentation with casual sex.[2]

This observation is commonplace, offered by writers of widely varying political outlooks. Describing the hookup culture found these days on many college campuses in the United States, Kathleen Bogle explained that women's experiences are often quite different from those of men:

Many of the women I interviewed had a story similar to Raquel's: a woman who was involved, sexually and otherwise, with a man often wanted that man to be in an exclusive relationship with her. When the two parties were not on the same page, women struggled with whether to "hang on" with the hope of a happy ending or to "move on" and start searching for a new partner. These women found it very difficult to end a relationship, even when they were not satisfied with its quality. For college women this sometimes came in the form of booty-call relationships or repeat hookup relationships.[3]

One part of an interview was particularly revealing for the overall results of the sexual revolution – specifically on college campuses but by implication for the culture as a whole:

ROBERT: It almost seems like [the hookup scene] is a guy's paradise. No real commitment, no real feeling involved, this is like a guy's paradise. This age [era] that we are in I guess.
KB [KATHLEEN BOGLE]: So you think guys are pretty happy with the [hookup] system?
ROBERT: Yeah! I mean this is what guys have been wanting for many, many years. And women have always resisted, but now they are going along with it. It just seems like that is the trend.[4]

Thus, the sexual revolution held out the promise that, with the pill and a "progressive" attitude to sex, women could now experience sex the way some men always had been able to in the past. What the culture of the sexual revolution could not deliver,

---

[2] Danielle Crittenden, *What Our Mothers Didn't Tell Us* (New York: Simon and Schuster, 1999), 31.
[3] Kathleen Bogle, *Hooking Up: Sex, Dating, and Relationships on Campus* (New York: New York University Press, 2008), 177.
[4] Ibid., 183.

however, was the same dualistic detachment in women from their bodies that many promiscuous males had seemed able to achieve (to their own detriment, we submit, but lay that aside for now). This fact is evidenced by the dramatic increase in emotional problems, suicides, self-mutilation ("cutting"), and eating disorders among young women.[5] As the social scientist Sheetal Malhotra, discussing such practices, indicated, "early sexual activity and multiple partners are also associated with pain and suffering from broken relationships, a sense of betrayal and abandonment, confusion about romantic feelings, altered self-esteem, depression, and impaired ability to form healthy long-term relationships."[6] So, while the culture in many ways suggests that sexual activity need have no profound consequences and is of itself meaningless – though able somehow to be transformed by choice into something meaningful – the experience of many women and men has been quite different.

Something similar has occurred regarding marriage, namely, a dramatic change in our culture's perception of it combined with serious concrete problems in reality. Fifty years ago, it was viewed as a *conjugal union*, that is, a specific type of bodily and spiritual union of complementary persons oriented to procreation and education of children. It was generally thought that marriage has an objective structure, that, while people are free to marry or not, people are not free to change marriage's basic structure. This was why marriage was believed to be for life, the kind of relationship that requires permanence. Also, marriage was viewed as intrinsically linked to procreation – as the kind of relationship that is characteristically fulfilled by having and raising children. However, in the last few decades, a different idea of "marriage" has become influential, namely, that it is basically an emotional tie that can be shaped in different ways by choice.

---

[5] Please note that we are not asserting that every case of each of these pathologies is caused by sexual promiscuity.

[6] Sheetal Malhotra, "Impact of the Sexual Revolution: Consequences of Risky Sexual Behaviors," *Journal of American Physicians and Surgeons* 13, no. 3 (2008): 89.

Several important changes in the institution of marriage indicate this shift in viewpoint.

First, the divorce rate in America has dramatically risen in the last fifty years. In fact, the rate of divorce is nearly twice what it was fifty years ago. "The average couple marrying for the first time now has a lifetime probability of divorce or separation somewhere between 40 and 50 percent."[7] This fact suggests that marriage is now viewed with less seriousness than previously.

Second, a significantly higher percentage of men and women today, as compared to fifty years ago, are opting for cohabitation as opposed to marriage. Sociologists conclude that between 1960 and 2009, the number of cohabiting couples in the United States has increased more than fifteenfold. Today about one-fourth of unmarried women age twenty-five to thirty-nine are living with a sexual partner, and an additional one-fourth have lived with a sexual partner (without marriage to that partner) at some time in the past.[8]

Third, there is a strong trend toward disconnecting marriage and child rearing. Fewer women are having children: in 1960, the birthrate (the average number of births per woman during her lifetime) was 3.65; today the birthrate in the United States is down to 2.09 (just about the replacement level), while in many other countries, it is even lower – in some cases, much lower. For example, in Germany, Spain, Italy, Greece, and Japan, the number is closer to 1. The separation between marriage and procreation in our culture is also shown by the dramatic increase in the percentage of children born outside marriage – to single or cohabiting parents. Since 1960, the percentage of children born to unmarried mothers has increased more than eightfold; in 2009, more than four in ten births were to unmarried mothers.[9] The percentage of children growing up in single-parent families or stepfamilies has grown enormously in the last fifty years.

---

[7] W. Bradford Wilcox and Elizabeth Marquardt, eds., *The State of Our Unions, 2010* (Charlottesville, VA: National Marriage Project, 2010), 71, http://www.stateofourunions.org/.

[8] Ibid., 76.

[9] Ibid., 95.

Fourth, although the traditional conception did not deny the desirability of emotional closeness in marriage, there was an emphasis on the idea that marriage involved a durable bond and that it normally enlarged into family. By contrast, there is a growing tendency in the last fifty years to view the central point of marriage to be emotional intimacy. (Vows composed by brides and grooms tend to emphasize emotions rather than marriage as an objective state or bond.) As Bradford Wilcox explains, over the last several decades, many Americans have moved away from an "institutional" model of marriage (which seeks to integrate sex, parenthood, economic cooperation, and emotional intimacy in a permanent union) to a "soul mate" model. On this model, marriage is seen "as primarily a couple-centered vehicle for personal growth, emotional intimacy, and shared consumption that depends for its survival on the happiness of both spouses."[10]

Many Americans believe that any relationship worth calling "marriage" must have an emotional closeness or emotional match. Hence the idea that spouses sometimes "just grow apart" and that, when this occurs, the marriage has "died" – an idea assisted by no-fault divorce laws – is part of the contemporary conception of marriage. Thus, whereas there is more freedom regarding marriage in one respect (with respect to its structure), there is less freedom regarding marriage in another respect – regarding its existence, since a large number of couples no longer feel themselves able to commit their future selves to marriage as a durable bond and so are not actually free to vow marriage "until death do [they] part" (for no one can guarantee emotional intimacy for a lifetime).

These points reflect a dramatic change in people's idea of what marriage is and of its purposes and norms. Fifty years ago, the predominant notion of marriage was that it is a conjugal union that men and women can choose to enter but whose structure they cannot alter. Today there is a strong trend toward viewing the structure of marriage as negotiable. Many view marriage as a construct that is created by its participants and shaped in its

[10] Ibid., 38.

meaning and norms by their subjective purposes and desires. A concrete sign of this is how brides and grooms approach their wedding vows. Fifty years ago, the traditional wedding vows were recited in nearly all weddings:

> I, John, take you, Mary, to be my wife, to have and to hold from this day forward, for better or for worse, for richer, for poorer, in sickness and in health, to love and to cherish; from this day forward until death do us part.

These vows convey the idea that although marriage begins only with the spouses' consent, that consent is given to enter into a state that has an objective structure and is of itself meant to be lifelong. By contrast, today it is not uncommon for brides and grooms to compose their own vows and deviate significantly from the historical norm.

These changes in how sexual activity and marriage are experienced and understood raise several vital ethical questions: Does sex have by its nature a profound importance, or can it be meaningful or not simply dependent on the intentions of the parties involved? If sexual activity does have an inherent profundity, what moral implications does this – together with basic moral principles – have? What is marriage? Does marriage have an objective structure, and if so, what is that structure? How, if at all, is marriage related to procreation and the rearing of children? Is there an intrinsic link, whether direct or indirect, between marriage and procreation? Is marriage permanent, or at least, should marriage be permanent – should marriage really be "for better or for worse, for richer, for poorer, until death do us part"? Is marriage exclusive, or can marriage exist between a man and several wives, or a wife and several husbands, or by groups of three or more in polyamorous sexual ensembles? Is sex outside marriage necessarily wrong? Is marriage necessarily between a man and a woman? What should the law say about marriage? Should our society redefine marriage, at least as a legal entity, to include same-sex partners? Should it include polyamorous groups of persons? What should the law be with respect to divorce?

Of course, many of these questions are addressed by various religious bodies and creeds. But in this book, we examine these issues from the standpoint of reason unaided by faith; that is, we do not presuppose here any revealed source of truth – we do not presuppose the truth of any sacred writings or the teachings of any authoritative religious body. The arguments we propose are ones that can be accepted by anyone, without regard to religious conviction and commitment. Thus, we will set out philosophical arguments (sometimes called "natural law" arguments) to defend traditional morality on the questions of what marriage is; whether it should be exclusive, permanent, between a man and a woman, and restricted to two persons, not three or more; whether sexual acts outside marriage are morally right; and whether marriage should be defined by the political community as an exclusive union of husband and wife.

Our approach is distinct from the approaches of many others who defend traditional sexual morality. In Chapter 2, we clarify the ethical approach we commend by distinguishing it from some inadequate arguments often advanced in support of traditional sexual morality, on one hand, and from hedonistic arguments advanced to defend a liberationist sexual ethic, on the other.

Chapter 3 explains what marriage is, both as a community and as an institution, and criticizes competing views. We show that marriage is the community formed by a man and a woman who publicly consent to share their whole lives, on every level of their being, including the bodily, in a type of relationship that would be fulfilled by begetting, nurturing, and educating children together (even if in fact this or that marriage does not result in children). In this chapter, we also show that marriage is by its nature exclusive and binding until the death of one of the spouses.

Chapter 4 sets out our argument for the proposition that sexual acts outside marriage are objectively immoral. Our argument centers on the choice to engage in a nonmarital sexual act and the relationship between this choice, on one hand, and what is genuinely fulfilling for the persons involved in that act, on the other hand. We argue that loving marital intercourse embodies marital communion and that it consummates or renews the marriage, that is, the two-in-one-flesh union of a man and a woman. And we argue that if sexual acts do not consummate or renew marriage, they involve a violation of the basic human good of marriage itself.

In Chapter 5, we consider how the law should view marriage. Here we examine the claim that marriage should be redefined to include same-sex and polyamorous unions and reject that claim. We also argue that the law should set forth the permanence of marriage as the norm and therefore that the laws that grant no-fault divorces should be repealed.

2

Human Nature and Morality

Sooner or later, in any discussion of the ethics of sex, the following argument – in its basic outlines – will be encountered: "Sodomy, masturbation, and (perhaps) all sex outside marriage are *unnatural* and, for precisely that reason, morally wrong." This is a *naturalist* approach. There are variations within this approach, but its central idea is that the nature of a human being just *is* the criterion to distinguish morally right from wrong in sexual matters.

Diametrically opposed to this approach is hedonism on sexual issues. According to this view, there is nothing special about sexual acts – other than the intensity of the pleasure and feeling they produce – and no distinctive ethical norms applicable to them. Moreover, the fact that an activity will bring pleasure, or enjoyable experience (which may include more than just physical pleasure), is a perfectly legitimate and worthwhile reason to perform that activity. So on this view, as long as sexual activity is consensual and not overridden by bad consequences (the transmission of disease, for example), it is morally permissible. In this chapter, we show why these views are mistaken and sketch a basic moral theory distinct from naturalism by which to evaluate choices, including those in the sexual domain.

The Unnatural Acts Argument

The naturalist argument mentioned previously is that certain actions, such as homosexual acts, are wrong because they are unnatural. More explicitly, the sexual power is reproductive by its nature – it is naturally oriented toward the kind of acts that could in some circumstances cause a child to be conceived – and so acts that could not in any circumstances result in procreation are unnatural. And to act in an unnatural manner is morally wrong. Let us call this the *unnatural acts argument*.

Unnatural in this argument could mean different things. It could mean "not in accord with nature." On this interpretation, the nature of a human being, including his or her basic natural powers, capacities, or faculties, provides a pattern according to which human beings should act. Deviations from this pattern, or patterns, are unnatural and therefore morally wrong. Thus, the natural sexual act has the male-female pattern, so sexual acts that deviate from this pattern are morally wrong.

Alternatively, *unnatural* could mean "contrary to nature." On this interpretation, an act that negates, or makes impossible the attainment of, an end to which a natural power is oriented is unnatural and therefore immoral. Because sex is naturally oriented to procreation – though that need not be viewed as the only good to which the sexual capacity is naturally oriented – acts chosen that thwart procreation or render it impossible are immoral. So, homosexual conduct, masturbation, and bestiality, among other kinds of sexual acts, are immoral.

Thomas Aquinas is widely interpreted as having presented an argument of this type when he spoke of "sins against nature" (which included masturbation, homosexual sodomy, and sodomy in opposite-sex couples), contending that such acts are "contrary to the natural order of sexual acts belonging to the human species."[1] Just as each nature is inherently oriented to a

---

[1] Aquinas, *Summa Theologiae*, 2.154.11. But for an interpretation that Aquinas's arguments on this issue are more subtle than is generally supposed, see John Finnis, *Aquinas: Moral, Political, and Legal Theory* (New York: Oxford University Press, 1998), 143–54.

certain end, so each power has its proper end. To violate the order of that power to its proper end is contrary to the human good and thus immoral. In one place, Aquinas said that the emission of semen is naturally oriented to procreation, so to emit semen in such a way that procreation is per se impossible (i.e., impossible in virtue of the kind of act performed, as opposed to the circumstances of the act) is contrary to the human good. "It is evident from this that every emission of semen, in such a way that generation cannot follow, is contrary to the good for man. And if this be done deliberately, it must be a sin."[2] Thus, according to this argument, the wrongness of these immoral acts – masturbation, sodomy, and so on – seems to be located first in the external act's relation to human nature (and secondarily in the will's choice of an act with such a defect).[3] (We hasten to add that in his treatise on natural law itself, and his treatise on marriage, Aquinas sets out a quite different, and in our judgment more cogent, approach.)

There are several problems with this argument. In the first place, it is not obvious that acting unnaturally is always morally wrong. On one hand, if human nature is viewed as a pattern, then it is not clear that deviating from that pattern is necessarily morally wrong. As Igor Primoratz (who himself adopts a hedonist position on sexual ethics) argues, "For it is not at all obvious that whatever is natural, i.e., biologically functional, is *ipso facto* morally good or required, and the other way around."[4] If a basic power is naturally oriented to an intrinsic good *A*, then to use it for the sake of realizing *B* instead of *A* does not seem in itself wrong or harmful. On the face of it, if that were all that was going on, that would seem to be simply a case of ingenuity rather than a case of violating a basic good. Of course, while one is

[2] Aquinas, *Summa Contra Gentile*, 3.122.5.
[3] If this argument were correct, it would follow that a doctor's pressing on a man's prostate gland to express semen for therapeutic reasons or to obtain a semen sample would be intrinsically immoral. Yet clearly the doctor's act is a morally different type of act than extramarital sexual acts such as fornication and masturbation.
[4] Igor Primoratz, *Ethics and Sex* (New York: Routledge, 1999), 53.

using the power or bodily part for *B*, one is then not realizing *A* (the good to which the power or part is naturally oriented); still, that by itself does not seem to render an act morally wrong, because the failure to realize an intrinsic good does not seem to be in itself, or at all times, morally wrong.

On the other hand, if an act is said to be *against* nature – and not just deviating from it – then it is still not obvious that it is necessarily morally wrong. Might one act contrary to a natural power for the good of the whole? Or might one act *against* the natural or the typical order of a power to its end, but still not harm or act against even the good to which that power is naturally oriented? For example, thwarting the nutritive power (the capacity of an animal to nourish itself) is in many cases – though obviously not in all – a healthy thing, not something contrary to the larger good of health. The capacity for nourishing is directly oriented toward converting external materials into energy sources and parts of the organism, but it is one of a number of capacities oriented to the basic and more complex good of health, which is the harmonious psychosomatic functioning of the organism as a whole. Thwarting the goal of the nutritive power need not be contrary to the basic good of health and does not seem always to be wrong.

There seem to be many instances of thwarting a natural power that are not morally wrong. For example, would it have been wrong when first learning about the nature of digestion to induce vomiting in a volunteer? Is it morally wrong for a lactating mother to express excess milk and then discard it? In both of these cases, it seems that one is using a natural power (the nutritive or lactating capacities) but then thwarting its natural orientation. And yet these acts do not seem morally wrong.

The naturalist ethicist may not give up here. He might argue that human nature is an expression of the Creator's will. He might say, first, that God created human nature, and, second, as a consequence, the patterns or directions within human nature are as it were commands from God the Creator, and so we are bound, after all – so the argument would go – to keep within the boundaries set by human nature, or we are bound to act in accord with, rather than against, human nature.

But this argument is unsuccessful. Although we are happy to agree that moral norms ultimately derive from God's wisdom, and are part of his providential order for creation, this argument fails. It implies that one's knowledge of any moral truth depends on knowing – at least implicitly – that God exists and directs us by creating human nature. Yet, it seems clear that one can arrive at conclusions regarding many moral questions – including on sexual issues – independently of one's acceptance of God's existence or of divine revelation.[5] So, even if one holds – either on faith or by philosophical argument – that God exists and that God orders the whole of creation (as we hold), still, one's knowledge of what is right and wrong is not logically dependent on one's knowledge that God exists and is provident. It is true that once one does know that an action is right, then, given that God exists and has a plan for his creation, it is reasonable to understand moral truth as directives from God the Creator. Our point is that one need not first know that a moral proposition is a directive from God before knowing that it is true and has a directive or prescriptive force. That God commands or prohibits a type of action does not figure *as a premise* in one's natural knowledge that such an action is morally required or morally wrong.[6]

Moreover, let us suppose that God exists and that he is the author of human nature. Still, it does not follow from these points alone that God wills that we must ensure that our actions always have the same patterns as our human nature or are always in accord with the orientations in each of our natural powers. Thus, from the fact that an act is not in accord with the teleology of a natural power, or that it thwarts an end of a natural

---

[5] The arguments in this book do not logically depend on any teaching from a divine revelation: just as we can know that stealing and rape are wrong before looking to revelation, just so, we argue, with the basic positions defended in this book.

[6] Of course, if one accepts that the Bible, or the teaching of the Church, for example, is a divine revelation, then one could discover a moral truth from the authority of this teaching. And so holding that something is wrong because it violates the Ten Commandments, for example, can be a reasonable position. But our argument in this book is philosophical in nature and does not presuppose any act of faith.

power, it does not follow that it is against God's will or that it is immoral.

The naturalist argument just examined emphasizes our human nature as a pattern and must appeal to the divine will to provide obligatory force to adhere to that pattern. But a different defense of naturalism for traditional sexual ethics can be advanced. Instead of viewing human nature as a pattern, this approach emphasizes human nature's inherent orientation to ends or purposes. It makes use of Aristotle's argument that the good of a thing consists in the exercise of its distinctive *function*. The basic ethical argument in sex ethics, we are told, is a simple application of Aristotelian–Thomistic metaphysics to the question of what distinguishes good human actions from bad ones. Thus, Edward Feser confidently asserts, "The point I want to emphasize is that, far from having no rational basis, the moral views now associated in the secularist mind with superstition and ignorance in fact follow inexorably from a constant application of the metaphysical ideas we've traced back through Aquinas and the other Scholastic thinkers to Plato and Aristotle."[7]

This argument to establish the basic moral criterion is as follows. To say that a thing is *good* is simply to say that it has the fullness of being due the kind of thing it is, that is, that it fulfills its nature. So, *human* goodness will consist simply in the fulfillment of human nature, that is, the attainment of the ends to which the various potentialities of human nature are oriented. Human beings have potentialities to understand what is true, to keep themselves healthy by self-nourishment, exercise, and other activities. So, understanding and healthful actions are good, whereas actions contrary to those ends – obfuscation and self-mutilation, for example – are bad. Actions that fulfill our nature are good; actions that impede or frustrate the orientation of our nature to its fulfillment are bad. Applied to sex ethics, this approach emphasizes the ends or purposes of our nature rather than our nature viewed as a pattern.

---

[7] Edward Feser, *The Last Superstition: A Refutation of the New Atheism* (South Bend, IN: St. Augustine's Press, 2008), 132.

The next step in this argument is the biological point that the human sexual capacity is naturally oriented to procreation (though there is no claim that this is its *only* natural purpose). Feser expresses this point succinctly: "Since the final cause [natural end] of human sexual capacities is procreation, what is good for human beings in the use of these capacities is to use them only in a way consistent with this final cause or purpose."[8] And from this it follows that sodomy, masturbation, fornication, and so on, are morally wrong. Like the previous defense of a naturalist approach, on this view, too, one argument by itself excludes almost all the sexual vices.

This argument appears to derive a moral ought (one ought not exercise the sexual capacity inconsistently with its natural end) from propositions describing human nature (the nature of the sexual capacity is oriented toward procreation), and the definition of good as that to which an entity is naturally oriented, or, equivalently, the exercise of an entity's function. And so it seems to commit what has come to be called the naturalistic fallacy, namely, deriving a moral-ought conclusion from premises all of which are is-propositions (i.e., descriptive propositions). But proponents of this approach reply that it *does* argue in that fashion, but to do so is not a fallacy at all; the idea that it is a fallacy is based on ignorance of the rich Aristotelian–Thomistic understanding of natures, or, equivalently, forgetting that *good* is a function-concept. Because natures are actually dynamic, oriented toward ends or purposes, it follows that *oughts* or *values* are already contained within natures: there can be no "wall of separation" between "is" and "ought" or between facts and values. As Feser puts it:

Well, there *is* such a problem [a naturalistic fallacy] if, as modern philosophers have done, one denies the reality of formal and final causes. But for those who avoid this foolish and ungrounded denial – such as Aristotle and Aquinas – there is no problem at all.[9]

[8] Ibid., 145.
[9] Ibid., 139.

In other words, once one understands that natures and natural capacities have dynamic orientations to ends, or, to use Aristotelian language, once one recognizes that they have *functions*, then one can see that the naturalistic fallacy is not actually a fallacy and the is–ought problem not actually a problem. Although Alasdair MacIntyre has not applied this argument to the sexual domain (as far as we know), and it is not clear even that he believes one can know with certainty what the human being's actual function is (or functions are), he explains well the central claim that the alleged naturalistic fallacy is not a fallacy:

> Hence any argument which moves from premises which assert that the appropriate criteria are satisfied to a conclusion which asserts that "That is a good such-and such," where "such-and-such" picks out an item specified by a functional concept, will be a valid argument which moves from factual premises to an evaluative conclusion. Thus we may safely assert that, if some amended version of the "No 'ought' conclusion from 'is' premises" principle is to hold good, it must exclude arguments involving functional concepts from its scope.[10]

Just as from the fact that the function of a watch is to tell time and the fact that this watch does not tell time, one can validly infer that this is a bad watch, so – provided one can know a human being's function, or functions – from the fact that a human being's function is X, and the fact that he or she does X or the fact that he or she does something contrary to X, it follows that he or she is doing something good or doing something bad.[11] As Feser explains, "Just as a 'good squirrel' is one that successfully carries out the characteristic activities of a squirrel's life by gathering acorns, scampering up trees, etc., so too a good human being is one who successfully carries out the characteristic activities of *human* life, as determined by the final causes or natural ends of the various faculties that are ours by virtue of our nature or essence."[12]

---

[10] Alasdair MacIntyre, *After Virtue*, 3rd ed. (Notre Dame, IN: University of Notre Dame Press, 2007), 58.
[11] Ibid.
[12] Feser, *Last Superstition*, 137n1.

However, this approach does not sufficiently heed the difference between theoretical reasoning (thinking about what is the case) and practical reasoning (thinking about what is to be done – primarily about what one is to do but, secondarily, in a hypothetical manner, about what it would be good to do). A theoretical proposition is true if it conforms to what is the case – including what could be the case, or what would have been the case given certain conditions. The point of asserting a theoretical proposition – precisely in that assertion – is to conform one's mind to what is the case.[13] By contrast, the point of asserting a practical proposition is to order or specify action (either actually or hypothetically). This is why a theoretical proposition cannot just by itself imply a practical proposition, nor can two or more such propositions by themselves imply a practical proposition.

Feser's and MacIntyre's arguments confuse the notion of good as a theoretical notion with the notion of good as a directive. Here's the way their basic arguments are supposed to work:

Every act that fulfills human nature is *good*.

X is an act that fulfills human nature.

Therefore, X is (so far forth) *good*.

The problem is that the term *good* in the premise has the theoretical meaning "what contributes to the fullness of being that is due a thing," or something along those lines. However, for the argument to establish a normative conclusion, the term must have, not its theoretical sense, but its *practical* sense, namely, "something fulfilling *that is to be done or pursued*" (and the term will have a practical meaning through its being part of a practical *proposition*). For if the meaning of the conclusion were merely "X contributes to the fullness of being that is due a (human) being,"

---

[13] We add the phrase "precisely in that assertion" because a theoretical assertion can be part of a practical inference. For example, in the inference *One ought to avoid what is unhealthy, smoking is unhealthy, therefore one ought to avoid smoking*, the second premise is theoretical – the point of that assertion, just by itself, is to state what is the case, although this occurs as part of a larger, practical inference.

then we would need to add a proposition to reach the properly practical or normative proposition: one would need the properly practical proposition "that which contributes to the fullness of being that is due a (human) being is *to be done or pursued.*"

This point can be illustrated perhaps more clearly by looking at the type of syllogism that is supposed to prove that an action should *not* be done. The naturalist's argument would be along these lines:

Whatever impedes the fulfillment of one's nature is bad.

Y impedes the fulfillment of one's nature.

Therefore, Y is bad.

Again, this is a valid syllogism, but only if the term *bad* in the conclusion is taken in a theoretical sense rather than a practical sense. If *bad* means simply "what has or causes a privation," then the conclusion is that "Y is what has or causes a privation." But, in order that the premises provide evidence for a *practical* proposition, one would need to add the following proposition: "what has or causes a privation *is to be avoided.*" The same point applies if, instead of using the term "fulfillment of one's nature," one uses the term "is an exercise of one's function." And the same problem occurs with the negative inference, if one uses the term "what impedes the exercise of one's function." So, there must be a normative proposition within the premises. One cannot simply deduce from Aristotelian, Thomistic, or Scholastic metaphysics a master ethical principle for ethics or sexual ethics.

One might argue that one can infer what ought to be done from what is, because whether an action is such as to help an agent realize its natural end, that is, the actualization of its given potentialities, is a matter of fact, a matter of what is the case. But whether an action helps realize an agent's end is the same as whether this action is morally right or wrong. However, although it is true that the relation of various means to ends is a relation that can be known by theoretical (as opposed to practical) reasoning – that is, it is a matter of fact or of what-is, not just of what-ought-to-be-done – still, such a relation will indicate what ought to be done only if one presupposes that the end *ought to be pursued*. And the knowledge of the basic ends to be pursued, we maintain, is realized in a practical insight, not an inference from theoretical propositions (propositions stating what is the case).

Another significant problem with the naturalist argument is that it either reduces morally good action to a mere means in relation to the agent's nonmoral perfection or it begs the question. For, on the naturalist view, one is supposed to discover, prior to practical insight, what the perfection of the human being is, and this knowledge is supposed to provide the goal or goals of human action. But the fulfillment of a human being either includes distinctive moral goodness or it does not. If it does not, then morally good action is merely instrumental in relation to nonmoral fulfillment; if it does, then the idea of the complete fulfillment of the human being *presupposes* an awareness of moral goodness, and its criterion, and so the argument begs the question. Naturalist thinkers may be expected to oscillate between the two options. And so moral actions are often viewed primarily as external actions that are *productive* of an external goal. In other words, the moral dimension of the human being is often reduced to the technical dimension – moral questions are often viewed as essentially questions about the efficiency of producing an external goal, in this case, the well-rounded human being. This problem can be seen in another way. The fact that an action realizes a basic capacity of a human being indicates that this action is a component of human fulfillment, a real human good. But this point by itself does not show how the will should be related to this human good, or to the human goods in general, which is the specifically ethical question.

Some philosophers infer from the failure of naturalism (plus their view that Kantian attempts to ground a more restrictive sexual ethics also fail) that there are no objective moral norms specifically applicable to sexual acts. They contend that as long as sexual acts do not involve coercion or deception (and do not result in very bad consequences), the act should be viewed as permissible – with the result that nonmarital acts, casual sexual acts, and perhaps even commercial sexual acts (prostitution) can often be morally permissible.[14]

However, we argue later that the distinction between what is morally right and morally wrong *is* based on the nature of human persons, but not in the way naturalism holds. Neither human nature itself, viewed as a pattern, nor the ends of our basic capacities, viewed as products, constitute the moral criterion. Rather, we argue, the basic moral criterion directs us *to choose* in a way that is in line with a will toward integral human well-being and fulfillment, namely, a love for, and openness to, all of the basic, irreducible aspects of human flourishing (both in ourselves and in others).

Basic Human Goods and Practical Principles

We begin by analyzing what occurs in a typical choice, and in the deliberation preceding a choice. Virtues, life plans, and life narratives are important, but they are constituted or formed by choices.[15] *Moral* goodness or badness is the goodness or badness precisely of acts of will and primarily of choices (including also the goodness or badness of the actions that carry out those choices). Character traits such as virtues, vices, and omissions that are not chosen derive their moral quality from what we do actually choose. We argue that all choices respond to basic goods, the intrinsic aspects of human fulfillment, and that *how* our choices relate to the *whole* set of basic human goods – both in ourselves and in other persons – determines whether an action is morally right or wrong, whether we morally ought to make such a choice or not.

We human persons often find ourselves in situations in which we understand that there are different actions we could perform, and we understand something distinctively appealing or

---

[14] E.g., Primoratz, *Ethics and Sex*, Chapter 5.

[15] It is important to note also that some choices organize more of one's life than others, because some bear on relationships or statuses, are implemented by further, smaller choices, and are sometimes called commitments to signal their importance.

beneficial in each performance, but we cannot perform all of those actions. One could do *A* or one could do *B* (say, go to the gym and work out or go to the library and study). There is something intelligibly appealing about doing *A* and something appealing about doing *B*; that is, action *A* has some benefit in it (either in the action itself or in bringing about some benefit distinct from the action), and action *B* offers a different benefit; for example, by going to the gym, I will contribute to my health and perhaps converse with friends, and by going to the library, I will increase my understanding in study. I cannot simultaneously do both: I cannot be both in the gym and in the library at the same time. Also, the benefit or good realized by *A* is of a distinct kind from the benefit offered by *B*. And so, *A* does not offer everything appealing, or good, that *B* does plus more, or vice versa; each option offers something the other one does not offer.[16] These are the kinds of situations in which one needs to make a choice; one needs to direct oneself toward one option rather than the other (or, possibly, choose simply to refrain from acting – which, of course, is also a choice).

Even in situations in which one of the options is judged to be immoral, one chooses between possible actions, each of which offers some distinctive benefit or good – or at least seems to. If someone deliberates about committing adultery as opposed to going home to eat dinner, the immoral option of committing adultery occurs to him or her for serious deliberation only because it is appealing, only because it offers some actual or supposed benefit, such as pleasure, boost of self-esteem, and/or the experience (without the reality) of contributing to a personal

---

[16] The moral theory we sketch is often called the *new natural law theory*. For seminal sources, see Germain Grisez, Joseph Boyle, and John Finnis, "Practical Principles, Moral Truth and Ultimate Ends," *American Journal of Jurisprudence* 33 (1988): 99–151; John Finnis, Joseph M. Boyle Jr., and Germain Grisez, *Nuclear Deterrence, Morality and Realism* (Oxford: Oxford University Press, 1987), Chapters 9–11. John Finnis, *Fundamentals of Ethics* (Washington, DC: Georgetown University Press, 1983); Finnis, *Aquinas*; Robert P. George, *In Defense of Natural Law* (Oxford: Oxford University Press, 2001).

communion. And of course, going home to dinner, in addition to the benefits it offers of health (including safety!) and of building up one's spousal relationship, also offers the obvious benefit of not betraying the trust of, and commitment to, one's spouse.

Of course, in many cases, the benefit or good that is offered by the action is a merely instrumental good – for example, one earns money not for its own sake but for what it can buy, or at times one cooks dinner as a mere means to eating (though at other times one might see a benefit intrinsic to cooking, as an art or skillful performance). But not all goods can be merely instrumental. That is, in many cases, the benefit or good is only a way of realizing some further good, and that good a means to another, and so on; but the chain of such instrumental goods cannot be infinite. There must be ultimate reasons for one's choices, some goods that one recognizes as reasons for choosing that are not mere means to some further good. These goods we call *basic human goods*; they are sufficient to motivate one to act in order to realize or participate in them. They are recognized as being intelligibly choiceworthy for their own sakes, as opposed to being intelligible only as means to other ends.

What are these ultimate (in the sense of irreducible and there-fore basic) reasons for action, or basic human goods? Are they the same for all human beings, or do they vary from culture to culture or even from individual to individual? Some argue that the ultimate goods for the sake of which we act are simply objects we happen to desire, and that these may be quite different for different people, and different for the same person at different times. On this view, reason merely has the function of calculating the most efficient ways of realizing the ends that we just hap-pen to desire. In David Hume's famous phrase, reason is merely "the slave of the passions." We can call this the "satisfaction of desire" account, because the ultimate reasons for action are the satisfactions of desires, desires that may vary from individual to individual (and from one time to another in the same individual).

On another view – *hedonism* – the intrinsic goods that provide ultimate reasons for action are pleasures or enjoyable states of consciousness. Of course, on this view, the concrete objects or conditions that bring about these enjoyable conscious states may be different for different people (and so although hedonism is conceptually distinct from the satisfaction of desire account, their practical conclusions are very similar).[17]

The central problem with these positions, in our judgment, is that each of them puts the cart before the horse: an object is not judged to be good because it is desired; rather, it is desired because it is judged – rightly or wrongly – to be good. And an object is not actually good simply because it would cause enjoyment; rather, an object (a condition or activity) is reasonably enjoyed only if that object is truly good. A person might find himself or herself with a desire for an object he or she knows is *not* worthwhile. For example, the person may find himself or herself desiring to eat dirt (a medical condition called pica or geophagia) or even, through a neural quirk, plagued by a bizarre desire – for example, an overwhelming desire to count the number of the blades of grass on courthouse lawns.[18] These desires are obviously for conditions or activities that are not genuinely worthwhile. Desires are not self-validating. Objects of desires require some feature that makes them worthwhile and the desire for them reasonable. A similar point applies to pleasures: whether a pleasure is a genuine good depends on what one is taking pleasure in – the pleasure of a Nazi in murdering people whom he dislikes or the pleasure of a sadist, for example, is not a good. But if hedonism were true, one would have to say that the pleasures experienced by the Nazi or the sadist *were in themselves* goods, though outweighed by the pain or harm he causes. This is incorrect – such pleasures are not goods to begin with. Thus, whether a pleasure is a good, or a disorder, depends on what one takes pleasure in – whether the object of the pleasure is a genuine good.[19]

To salvage the idea that the satisfaction of desires is what makes something worthwhile, one may amend the simple desire

---

[17] See, e.g., Primoratz, *Ethics and Sex*.

[18] John Rawls cites this example in *Theory of Justice* (Cambridge, MA: Harvard University Press, 1978), 432.

[19] The conditional goodness of pleasure is treated in somewhat more detail in the second section of Chapter 4.

account by saying that the satisfaction of a desire is a good only if one *would have* the desire if one were fully informed of the consequences of its satisfaction and of its coherence (or lack of coherence) with other desires. On this amended version, what is good for a person, or a person's well-being, consists in the satisfaction of *ideal* desires rather than of the actual desires we happen to have. However, we can conceive of coherent sets of desires that are still oriented toward ways of life that are quite trivial or even bad (in the sense of miserable). If one has an over-arching desire to count the blades of grass on courthouse lawns, one could adjust one's other desires to produce a coherent set. Hence the coherence of a desire with other desires is insufficient to bestow value or worthiness on the object of that desire. A desire for an activity or condition – even a desire one *would* have only if it could be made coherent with other desires and one had full information about its consequences and other circumstances – is not good on the grounds that it would be desired in such ideal circumstances. Rather, the desire for it is a reasonable desire only if it is oriented toward an object that is truly good.

Hence the objects of our ultimate desires or interests must have a feature (or features) that makes those objects truly worth-while. And such a feature is grasped by reason or intellect – for what is grasped is a feature held in common by many conditions or activities. In our judgment, the classical tradition, including Plato, Aristotle, and Aquinas, is correct on this issue: the feature we apprehend that grounds the worthiness of an end is that it is genuinely *fulfilling* or *perfective* of us and of others like us. Our basic desires, that is, our basic volitions, are informed and specified by basic practical judgments. And these are recognitions that certain conditions, activities, ends, or purposes – such as life and health, understanding, skillful performance, or harmony with other people – are basic human goods, that is, aspects of true flourishing and, precisely as such, worth pursuing and promoting, both in ourselves and in others.

This is *not* to say that one first acquires a knowledge of what human nature is, or of the basic capacities and natural inclinations that are constitutive of human nature, and then infers moral oughts from that knowledge – an instance of the naturalistic fallacy, which, as we argued earlier, is indeed a fallacy. Rather, we grasp the goodness and choiceworthiness of the basic goods in *practical* propositions. A practical proposition is not a description; it is a *directive* or a *pre*-scription.

Nor are these basic practical judgments *intuitions* – intellectual acts without data. One first knows that life, knowledge, or friendship is a good to be pursued, by direct insight into natural tendencies toward such goods, into experiences of participating in and enjoying these goods, and perhaps also by contrast with deprivations of them. For example, as a young child, one experiences being healthy as opposed to being sick or having scraped-up knees. One *enjoys*, or *takes delight in*, being healthy, and one *dislikes*, or *has an aversion to*, being sick or wounded. But these experiences are not yet practical insights; such enjoyments or aversions are on the level of feeling or emotion – what Aristotle and Aquinas called *sense appetite*. However, at some point, even as a child, one goes further and one comes to *understand* that being healthy (exercising harmonious bodily and psychic functioning) is a good worth pursuing and promoting and that being sick or wounded is a harm to be avoided. What has been achieved is a practical insight, a rational apprehension that being healthy is an aspect of human flourishing, worthy of pursuit and protection.[20] In a similar way, one comes to understand that knowledge itself a good worthy of pursuit, and the same for aesthetic experience, harmony with other people, and other basic human goods.

Basic Human Goods

As irreducible aspects of the well-being and fulfillment of human persons, the basic human goods are transcultural. It is true for all human beings, in all times and places, that health, knowledge, and friendship fulfill them, improve their lives, just of themselves,

---

[20] On the basis of this practical intellectual insight, one has a natural love for, or interest in, the intelligible good understood.

whereas sickness, ignorance, and alienation diminish them. And the same point applies to the other basic goods. Since all human beings have the same nature, the same basic potentialities, and the actualization of their basic potentialities (in a way that leaves open further actualization) is the real fulfillment or completion of the human person, it follows that the basic goods are the same for all human beings. (Of course, they can be realized and instantiated in very different ways, some of which reflect significant cultural differences.)

Since human beings are complex, there are many basic human goods. Because human beings are living bodily beings, physical organisms, they are perfected or fulfilled by *life and health*. As rational or intellectual beings, human beings are perfected by understanding and *knowledge of truth* and *aesthetic experience*. As both bodily and intellectual, human beings are fulfilled in doing and making things, that is, *skillful performances of many different types*. As complex beings, human beings are fulfilled by the harmony of the different aspects of the self, harmony of the bodily and the spiritual, and of the emotional, volitional, and intellectual acts. This basic good can be called *self-integration, inner harmony,* or *integrity*. As creatures who form relationships with other human beings – and not merely for instrumental reasons or to more efficiently realize individualistic goals – human beings are fulfilled by *friendship and society*. In every culture, people seek to establish or maintain a harmony between themselves and more-than-human sources of meaning and value in the universe – with fate, the gods or God; this is the good of *religion*.

Finally, as sexually complementary persons, human beings are able to create a unique community, which normally includes handing on human life; and this is the basic human good of *marriage*. We say much more about marriage as a distinctive basic good in the next chapter. But let us note here that people often are motivated to marry, simply because they wish to spend their lives together and, they hope, build a family: their marriage is an intelligible good providing a sufficient rational motive for their choice. Moreover, it is not only a specific type of friendship – though it includes that; because it involves a bodily union, as well as an emotional, volitional, and intellectual union, it is distinct from the basic good of friendship. Finally, not everyone need be married to participate in certain ways in this basic human good: one participates in it by being part of communities – one's own family, to begin with – that contribute to marriage (being a son or daughter, brother or sister, aunt or uncle, friend of married couples, etc.).

Each of these goods is distinct and irreducible; that is, each offers an aspect of flourishing not offered by the others (though the goods other than life presuppose it, and the goods consisting in harmony presuppose pursuit of such goods as life, health, knowledge, and skillful performance or play). Thus, being alive and healthy does not of itself realize the good of knowledge; excellence in work or play does not of itself realize the good of friendship – and similarly with the other basic goods.

Since each basic human good is an intrinsically good, distinct aspect of human fulfillment, and not a mere means toward the others, these basic goods cannot be measured against one another in terms of their goodness, which is to say they are, precisely in respect to that which makes them appealing – their goodness, that is, their being perfective of us – incommensurable.[21] There are many respects in which they can be measured against one another – for example, moral norms themselves are ways of measuring pursuits of various goods against one another, though moral norms properly measure the choices to pursue various goods, not the goods themselves. But they cannot be measured against one another with respect to their goodness as such. Things can be measured against one another only with respect to some feature they have in common. But since the goodness of each basic human good is not a part of or a means in relation to any other, it follows that their goodness itself, their perfectiveness, is not a common feature one can reasonably judge that one has

---

[21] Of course, each good can be pursued as a means of realizing others – knowledge for the sake of work, work for the sake of health, etc.; still, they *need not* be instrumental because each good in itself is a distinct aspect of human flourishing.

to a higher degree than another. Each basic human good is a way of being fulfilled, but each is an irreducibly distinct type of fulfillment.

Of course, goods extrinsic to the person are objectively inferior – precisely in respect to what makes them appealing – to goods intrinsic to the person. And some goods – such as religion, or, for people who are married, marriage itself – organize more of one's life than other goods and so are more architectonic. But the basic human goods are incommensurable with respect to that which makes them appealing to begin with, which is their being perfective or fulfilling. (They are, in specific circumstances of concrete choosing between options, often brought into a kind of commensurability by the application of moral norms that exclude certain possible choices despite the fact that those choices would enable the choosing subject to realize or participate in a basic human good.)

This is an important point for the study of sexuality and marriage. Knowledge and excellence in work are intrinsic basic goods. But so are human life and health, and marriage and family. Our culture tends to undervalue rearing children and work in the home. But it is a mistake, for example, to think that the world of work outside home or that of theoretical knowledge is of itself superior to domestic work (protecting health in children and building up family and marriage). Each of these goods is a distinctive aspect of human flourishing, irreducible and incommensurable in relation to the others.

The First Moral Principle

The first practical principles directing us to pursue knowledge, life, health, friendship, and so on, as intelligible purposes that fulfill us in one dimension of our being or another as human persons do not by themselves distinguish between morally right ways of pursuing these goods and morally wrong ways of doing so. That is because they are the source of all practical reasoning. Just as one cannot begin to figure out what road to take unless one sees some point in going somewhere, so one cannot begin to deliberate about what action to choose unless one first apprehends that there are some goods worth pursuing for their own sakes, and not merely as means to other ends. The intelligent awareness of the basic purposes of action – the ultimate reasons for action – is realized in the basic practical judgments just discussed. And so the first practical principles are operative both in reasoning that concludes to a morally bad choice and in reasoning that concludes to a morally good choice.

If both bad choices and good ones include pursuing basic human goods, then how can these basic goods distinguish between the morally good choices and the morally bad ones? The difference cannot be that morally good choices are oriented toward the right goal and morally bad ones are aimed at an evil goal. For morally bad choices also typically aim at some basic human good (such as health or community of a sort), or at least a part of a basic human good. Nor can the difference be that morally bad choices are oriented only toward apparent goods, whereas good choices aim at real goods, for in some immoral choices, a real good is pursued. For example, an unfair act, such as favoring one's close friend in a job selection, may involve pursuing a genuine good though unduly neglecting its realization in someone not near and dear to one. Nor can the difference be that morally bad choices are motivated by self-interest, whereas morally good ones are altruistic: one can make morally bad choices for others' sake, and proper love of self is not morally wrong (though *unfair* preference for oneself is morally wrong).

Still, the difference between the morally good and bad choices must be somehow grounded in the human good, the basic goods that provide more than merely instrumental reasons for our actions and fulfill us as persons. For, any moral criterion that was extrinsic to the human good would be seen as an external imposition. Moreover, if the moral good were not grounded in the human good itself, then the question would at some point arise, "Why should I be moral?" And if that question can intelligibly be raised, it cannot have an answer. The result would be paradoxical: one could not claim that we are unconditionally required to be moral. (Since the moral criterion is, in a way, the

basic goods themselves – as we explain in a moment – then the
moral criterion itself also provides a reason to follow it: following
it is doing the most reasonable thing.)

Of course, consequentialism – the position that one should
choose that option which overall and in the long run promises
to produce the net best proportion of benefit to harm – also is
a proposal that grounds the moral norm in human goods. But
we think there are insuperable problems for this theory of moral
assessment and judgment. First, consequentialism supposes that
the goods and bads (benefits and harms) in the options considered for deliberation can be objectively measured, so that it is
possible to say – prior to the application of moral norms, since
this measure is supposed to generate the moral norms – that one
option has all the good in it that the other option does, plus more
(or that one option has measurably less harm in it, if both options
would produce more harm than good). But this position cannot
be sustained. Usually there are different kinds of good (different forms of basic goods) at stake in the different options, and
that alone blocks measuring the goods and bads in the options
for choice. Moreover, even where that is not the case – say, the
different options involve different instances of the same kind of
good – the consequentialist proposal is unworkable. If the goodness or badness of options for choice *can* be measured against
one another – so that one can say that this option offers all the
good that the other one does, plus more – then it does not seem
that the option with the lesser good in it could be chosen at all.
It is possible to choose an option (a performance) only if it offers
some good or advantage not offered by the other option.[22] If
one option really does offer less than the other one – in the sense
that the other option offers every advantage offered by this one,
plus more – then what could be the point of choosing the lesser
option?

---

[22] Of course, if two options are not intelligibly different at all, then one will then
simply resort to some nonrational method of selecting one, such as choosing
the drink nearest to hand – but these are not morally significant choices, and
the point of a moral theory is precisely to enable people to resolve moral
questions in the most reasonable way.

Furthermore, the consequentialist method treats the basic goods of each person – including his or her own life – as only conditionally good, as if this person's inherent goodness and worthiness were dependent on his or her intrinsic fulfillment, including his or her very life, fitting into the larger reality of "the greatest good in the long run" or "the greatest good for the greatest number." And yet we begin our practical reasoning by recognizing the inherent goodness of each basic good, in each person.[23] Hence we reject the consequentialist moral criterion.

Rather, our suggestion is that the difference between a morally good and a morally bad choice is that a morally good choice is fully consistent with all of the practical principles (*life is a good to be pursued, knowledge is a good to be pursued*, etc.), whereas a morally bad choice is not fully in accord with all of these principles. A morally good choice is a fully reasonable choice; a morally bad choice is, in one way or another, to one extent or another, unreasonable. Of course, the practical principles are directives to the intrinsic goods of persons, both ourselves and others. So another way of stating the basic moral criterion is to say that a morally good choice is one that is in accord with the human good integrally understood, that is, a love and respect for all of the basic human goods, both in oneself and in others; a morally bad choice, in one way or another, *diminishes* or *suppresses* openness toward or respect for the intrinsic goods of persons. We begin with an interest in, or an appreciation of, the various basic human goods, in oneself and in others. A morally good choice *enhances* our respect for the basic goods; a morally bad choice diminishes that respect.

For example, in an unfair choice, one treats the intrinsic goods of some persons as being as such inferior to those of others – in effect, treating their fulfillment as if it were not intrinsically good. Or in a choice to destroy, damage, or impede one instance

---

[23] For more extended criticisms of consequentialism, see Finnis et al., *Nuclear Deterrence, Morality and Realism*, Chapter 9, and Patrick Lee, *Abortion and Unborn Human Life*, 2nd ed. (Washington, DC: Catholic University of America Press, 2010), Chapter 5.

of a basic good for the sake of other goods, one treats the good destroyed, damaged, or impeded as if it were good only as a part of a larger whole rather than as intrinsically good. In other words, the difference between morally good and morally bad choices is that the morally good choice is in accord with the *integral* directiveness of all of the basic human goods (in oneself and in others), and the morally bad choice falls short of that in some way, that is, introduces into one's will (one's basic capacity for responding to understood goods and harms) a privation of openness or respect for some instance of a basic good or some person. In one way or another, the morally bad choice departs from the choice that would be made by someone maintaining an appreciation of and respect for all of the basic goods. Thus, the basic moral principle is that one should choose entirely in accord with reason (i.e., fully in accord with all of the basic practical principles) or with all of the basic goods, both in oneself and in others.

This is just a sketch of a natural law theory. Still, it shows, first, that on a natural law theory, the basic moral criterion need not be conceived of as a set of limitations or as primarily negative. When the emphasis is placed on choices in relation to basic human goods, understood precisely as the intrinsic aspects of the fulfillment of human persons, then the affirmative moral norms logically come first before negative norms. The basic moral norm is to energetically pursue and promote the basic human goods both in oneself and in others. The prohibitions – such as do not intentionally kill innocent persons, do not steal, do not commit adultery – exclude choices and actions that are themselves negative.

Furthermore, this sketch shows that we are called to fashion by our free choices and commitments different forms of life, respectful and appreciative of the various intrinsic goods of persons. Morality does not prescribe the exact same type of life for us all; there is room for a great deal of diversity and ingenuity in living out morally good lives. For there are many basic human goods, and there is perhaps an infinite number of ways of realizing these various basic goods. We are not required to realize all the basic goods equally, or in the same order. We are called to fashion a life in which we energetically pursue some, and at all times respect all, of the intrinsic goods of all persons.

Some Implications of the First Moral Principle

The basic moral criterion is very general, but it has more specific implications. Germain Grisez, Joseph Boyle, and John Finnis have called these *modes of responsibility*.[24] For example, if one respects all of the basic human goods, then one will not allow hostility to lead one intentionally to harm someone (destroy, damage, or impede an instance of a basic human good in someone). Similarly, one will not allow fear that is not grounded in an intelligible concern for a real harm to deter one from pursuing a basic good or fulfilling one's duty: for example, one will not let the mere fear of pain deter one from visiting the dentist. Also, if one chooses in line with a love and respect for all the basic human goods, one will not allow an emotional desire for a pleasure not connected to a genuine good (in other words, a pleasure that is not the experiential aspect of realizing or participating in an intelligible good) lead one away from choosing a genuine good – for example, one will not allow a mere desire to feel a "high" lead one to become intoxicated, or the desire for the taste of chocolate to eat a candy bar if one is a diabetic. Again, one ought not to be deterred by languor or mere fear of work from pursuing a basic human good – for example, deliberately oversleeping and failing to meet certain responsibilities when one is not sick or in need of the extra sleep.

Finally, as we mentioned previously when discussing consequentialism, if one chooses in line with an appreciation and respect for all of the basic goods, one will not choose to destroy, damage, or impede one instance of a basic good to promote other

---

[24] E.g., Germain Grisez, *The Way of the Lord Jesus: Vol. 1, Christian Moral Principles* (Chicago: Franciscan Herald Press, 1983), Chapter 8; Grisez et al., "Practical Principles, Moral Truth, and Ultimate Ends"; John Finnis, *Natural Law and Natural Rights* (New York: Oxford University Press, 1980).

goods or to avoid bad consequences: the end does not justify the means. The point is, one should pursue the various basic human goods intelligently and not be misled by unintegrated emotion into choosing in a way that denigrates or unduly neglects an instance of an intrinsic basic good or some persons' share in basic goods.

In sum, the naturalist approach is mistaken in its claim that moral norms are deduced from propositions describing human nature. One cannot logically infer a moral ought from premises all of which express merely what-is. But the naturalist approach is correct to hold that moral norms are in some way grounded in human nature. The first practical principles and the first moral principle are not derived from theoretical propositions but arise out of direct insights into the possibilities toward which we are oriented by our human nature. These basic goods are aspects of genuine flourishing. The basic moral norm is that we should energetically pursue various basic goods and respect all of the basic goods, both in ourselves and in others, not being deterred from that respect by partiality, fear, emotional desire, and so on. Pleasure is not itself a basic good, but it is not wrong to pursue pleasure as an aspect of a genuine good. The pursuit of pleasure and enjoyment can mislead, however, if the pursuit of it – as just a sensation, or as unconnected to a larger good as its experiential aspect – leads us away from promoting or realizing a genuine good of someone or toward harming someone. From the first moral principle, other more specific moral norms follow. The ethics of sex and marriage will be concerned, not principally with patterns of external actions, nor with the most efficient way of attaining external ends, but with how our choices regarding sex and marriage relate to the basic goods at stake in this domain, namely, marriage itself and procreation.

3

What Marriage Is

There is, of course, profound disagreement today about what marriage actually is. The center of debate concerns how marriage is related to procreation and the rearing of children. Is marriage intrinsically related to having and rearing children, or is this only one of the benefits – or burdens – attached to some marriages, but only incidentally? In turn, this issue raises other questions: Is marriage only an emotional-spiritual relationship (or a union of hearts and minds), or instead, does it essentially include bodily union, sexual intercourse being a constituent part? Is marriage necessarily between a man and a woman, or can there be genuine same-sex marriages? Is marriage necessarily a union of two people, or can there be genuine marriages of three or more persons (triads, quadrads, etc.) in polyamorous sexual partnerships? Does marriage even have an objective structure, or instead, are its basic contours subject to the choice of the state or to the choices of individual couples? All of these questions concern what marriage is. Two further questions bear on attributes or properties of marriage (logical consequences of what marriage is): Is marriage inherently an *exclusive* bond, or may marriages be sexually "open"? Does marriage necessarily involve a sincere pledge of permanence, or may marriages be for set terms or "for as long as love lasts"?

Views of Marriage as Nonprocreative

It might seem that marriage cannot be intrinsically related to procreation and child rearing for the simple reason that many people
get married who are unable to conceive children together. Some
judges, at both the state and federal levels, have advanced this
argument against the proposition that marriage is intrinsically
related to procreation. When striking down Proposition 8 (which
reestablished conjugal marriage under California law after it had
been invalidated by that state's supreme court), Judge Vaughn
Walker curtly argued, "Never has the state inquired into procreative capacity or intent before issuing a marriage license; indeed, a
marriage license is more than a license to have procreative sexual
intercourse." And Chief Justice Margaret Marshall in her majority opinion in *Goodridge v. Department of Public Health*, the
Massachusetts Supreme Judicial Court ruling that struck down
that state's conjugal marriage law, advanced basically the same
argument. Replying to the contention that marriage's primary
purpose is procreation, Marshall confidently replied that

> this is incorrect... General Laws c. 207 contains no requirement that
> the applicants for a marriage license attest to their ability or intention
> to conceive children by coitus. Fertility is not a condition of marriage,
> nor is it grounds for divorce. People who have never consummated their
> marriage, and never plan to, may be and stay married.

In other words, since infertile couples can marry, procreation
(they argue) must be merely incidental to the concept and meaning of marriage.

If marriage lacks any inherent connection to procreation –
contrary to the position we defend – then what can marriage
be? That is, what does distinguish marriage from other types
of relationships? Different answers have been suggested (though
never elaborated). In the *Goodridge* case, Chief Justice Marshall
declared, "While it is certainly true that many, perhaps most,
married couples have children together (assisted or unassisted),
it is the exclusive and permanent commitment of the marriage
partners to one another, not the begetting of children, that is the
sine qua non of civil marriage." And earlier in the same opinion,

she wrote, "Civil marriage is at once a deeply personal commitment to another human being and a highly public celebration of the ideals of mutuality, companionship, intimacy, fidelity, and family." So, on this view, marriage is essentially a personal commitment, with the addition of stability and intimacy.

Conversely, a different view of what marriage is could be construed from statements made by Chief Justice Marshall earlier in that same opinion: "Civil marriage *is created* [emphasis added] and regulated through the exercise of the police power." And "while only the parties can mutually assent to marriage, the terms of the marriage – who may marry and what obligations, benefits, and liabilities attach to civil marriage – are set by the Commonwealth" (referring here to the state of Massachusetts). These passages suggest that marriage is only a *social construct*. That is, marriage is not a specific type of community, founded on the nature of human persons, with an objective structure, but an association constructed by society for its own purposes, one whose basic structure and contours are chosen by the state and subject to modifications introduced by the state. And of course, another possible view – though not one endorsed by the *Goodridge* majority opinion, as far as we can see – is that marriage is a relationship whose basic structure and contours are freely constructed *by individuals*, with the result that there could be many different core types of "marriage" within any given society.

Thus, when we ask about the fundamental structure of marriage, two issues arise: First, does marriage name a specific, objective reality? Or is marriage a mere social or individual construct? Second, if marriage does have an objective structure, is marriage intrinsically linked to having and raising children? Or is child rearing, where marriages include children, merely incidental to those marriages? We first examine how one can define a community and then show that marriage is distinguished from other communities in that it is a bodily as well as emotional and spiritual union that would naturally be fulfilled by the spouses conceiving and rearing children together. (This understanding also explains the principled basis of the norms governing

marriage – sexual exclusivity and fidelity, the pledge of permanence of commitment, the requirement of mutual care, come
what may – and accounts for the status of marriage as an intrinsic
human good and not merely something valuable as instrumental
to other goods, including the great good of having and rearing
children.)

Marriage: A Stable, Sexual Union, Apt for Procreation

Since marriage is a community, we must first clarify how a community can be defined and how it can have a definite structure
and require, as a matter of moral principle and not mere subjective preference, conduct and commitments that are essential
to that structure. As a first step, let us note that this is not just
a question about the meaning of a word. The kind of definition we seek is not merely semantic but the explanation of what
distinguishes this type of reality from others.

When we ask what something is, we typically begin with
paradigm instances picked out by some shared attributes indicating that several things might be of the same kind, and our
goal is to discover what fundamentally distinguishes these things
from others. We may end up discovering that some of the things
we thought were different in kind actually are not (for example, whales and apes are both mammals, although whales more
closely resemble fish at first glance), whereas others we thought
were the same in kind actually are not (e.g., gold and pyrite).
Of course, communities are not natural species, that is, kinds of
things that exist independently of human intervention, but are
formed by choices persons make to cooperate in various ways.
Still, since communities are formed by the common pursuit of
purposes, two communities will be essentially distinct if those
communities pursue different types of purposes or if they pursue
a common purpose in fundamentally different ways (e.g., one as
a mere means and the other as an end).

Thus, we can pick out instances of communities and ask what
they are. And if we arrive at an answer, we can then ask about
the ethical and political implications of such differences. Since the

forming of some communities is a way in which human beings are fulfilled, it follows that the way our choices are related to communities, and to the structures required by their purposes, is morally significant. For example, even generic friendship – that is, friendship not between spouses, and not founded on a quite specific connection such as paternity or the teacher-pupil relationship – has a structure definite enough so that some actions develop it and others harm it.

With respect to marriage, the central questions will be, Is there a specific and distinctive type of community picked out by the word *marriage*? Is there a distinctive common good or common purpose defining a distinctive kind of community? Or instead, does the word *marriage* pick out merely an arbitrary set (such as people with brown hair and under forty)?

In almost all cultures, we find instances of communities of the following sort: a union of a man and a woman formed by their commitment to share their lives – physically (including sexually), emotionally, and spiritually – in the kind of community that would be fulfilled by conceiving and rearing children together. This kind of community is traditionally called "marriage."[1] We refer to marriage, conceived in this way, as a *conjugal union* – denoting that the man and the woman have been joined together (the etymology indicates a common yoke) to make a new unit.

A union of this kind can come about in two ways: either primarily for the sake of the romantic union (and then the procreative orientation of the community is seen as the natural extension or culmination of their romantic union) or as the framework for procreation (and then the romantic union, or full union of the spouses, is seen as the suitable framework for the procreative orientation). So, a man and a woman may fall in love and then desire to be with each other, in fact, to become one with each

---

[1] We are not begging the question by beginning with opposite-sex couples as paradigm instances whose nature we seek to understand, for our method leaves open the possibility that same-sex couples might not actually differ in kind from the instances with which we begin. We do not presuppose here that the difference between opposite-sex and same-sex is more than incidental to the purpose of the community called marriage – that remains to be established.

other. Included in that desire, and giving shape to it, is a desire for bodily-sexual union. This desire to be one with each other on all levels of their being, including the sexual, distinguishes romantic or erotic love from other types of love. Marriage – the bodily, emotional, and spiritual union, of the kind that would be prolonged and fulfilled by procreation and the rearing of children together – answers to and fulfills romantic love.

Or the union of a man and a woman might be formed primarily as the suitable environment for children. In some cultures the union might even be arranged by parents before the bride and the groom love each other. And so the man and the woman decide to form a union oriented to having and raising children, but they also realize – or come to realize – that this union should not be a mere means to having and raising children. They realize that they should be united to each other – on the bodily, emotional, and spiritual level – for their own sakes, in the kind of communion whose culmination or prolongation is in conceiving and raising children together, though their union is good in itself.[2]

This type of relationship – whatever the initial motive for forming it – is fundamentally different from two other types of relationship, despite some similarities. First, some couples cohabit, and regularly have sex together, but view the possibility of having children as something extrinsic to their relationship. They may view having children as an attractive optional "extra" or merely as a burden to be avoided. But this is a distinct type of relationship, for the purpose of its ongoing cooperation is distinct from the communities mentioned earlier. In marriage, the union is specified by its procreative orientation – the spouses are united bodily, in an act that fulfills the behavioral conditions of procreation, and on other levels, in the kind of communion that is naturally extended by having and rearing children together. By contrast, in the latter type of community, if a child does come to

[2] There may, of course, be other extrinsic motives, such as economic reasons or status, for forming this union, but the union itself will be primarily aimed at romantic union or procreation, or both.

be from their sexual acts, the members in this relationship must then decide whether they will or will not form a new kind of union, one especially apt for and fulfilled by procreation.

Another type of relationship similar to marriage but fundamentally distinct from it is an alliance formed directly for the purpose of raising children. For example, two or more individuals may agree to cooperate for the sake of raising children – two widowed sisters, for example, or several celibate religious men or women. Though these relationships are, like marriage, oriented toward raising children, the way they are oriented toward that purpose is quite different. In marriage the spouses form a bodily, emotional, and spiritual union, and procreation and child rearing are the fruition of their union. By contrast, in this latter relationship, the union of the members of the community is a consequence of their decision to cooperate in the rearing of children. Since their union is not consummated (as it is in marriage) by sexual intercourse – more on that in a moment – theirs is not a *conjugal* union. No one would call these relationships marriages, and no society recognizes them as such.

Marriage and Sexual Intercourse

To understand further the distinctive nature of marriage, we must understand how sexual acts contribute to it. It is widely recognized that sexual acts between spouses in some way foster their marital unity or express their marital love. But it is seldom explained how that is so.[3] Some people say that sexual intercourse *signifies* or *symbolizes* mutual love. On this view, sexual intercourse is only a sign or symbol, and so it is distinct from, and thus extrinsic to, what it signifies or symbolizes. Indeed, this view is often proposed as a way of exalting marriage: proponents of this position often emphasize that marriage is a *spiritual*

---

[3] On this question, also see Sherif Girgis, Ryan T. Anderson, and Robert P. George, *What Is Marriage? Man and Woman: A Defense* (New York: Encounter Books, 2012).

union, much deeper than mere bodily realities, and that sexual intercourse is an apt sign or symbol, but not part of marriage itself.[4] Others hold that marriage is an emotional or spiritual union and that sexual acts foster it because they are mutual gifts of pleasure that intensify their mutual affection. But again, the bodily, sexual act is thought of as quite extrinsic to the marital union itself.

It is true that sexual intercourse is a sign or symbol. But it is much more than that. Indeed, it has a sign-value and can be a sign of love or commitment, precisely because of what it is *in reality*, before being a sign. When a man and woman make the decision to marry, they desire to be united – bodily as well as on other levels of their being. The sexual union of a man and a woman actualizes a real, biological union – a one-flesh union is an accurate description of it. Human beings are organisms, albeit of a particular type. In most actions – digesting, sensing, walking, and so on – individual male or female organisms are complete units. However, with respect to reproduction, the male and the female are incomplete. In reproductive activity – sexual intercourse – the male and the female participate in a single action, coitus, which is biologically oriented to procreation (though not every act of coitus actually reproduces), so that the *subject* of the action is the male and the female *as a unit*. Sexual intercourse is a unitary action in which the male and the female complete one another and become biologically one, a single organism with

---

4 Some contemporary, "personalized" wedding vows emphasize that one's bride or groom is not just one's spouse but one's *soul mate*. Of course, marriage does involve a union of souls, but what marriage is – the essence of marriage – includes bodily union as well. Indeed, a sound understanding of marriage presupposes a firm rejection of any dualistic understanding of human persons as souls (or minds) and not bodies – an understanding that reduces the body to the status of a subpersonal extrinsic instrument at the service of the soul (or mind), considered as the "true" person. Persons are soul (or mind)-body composites. Human beings are not properly understood as nonbodily persons inhabiting (or in some mysterious way associated with) nonpersonal bodies. Persons are souls (or minds) and bodies. When persons are united in marriage, they are united as soul mates, yes, but as bodies as well – they become "one flesh."

respect to this function (though, of course, not with respect to others). Just as an individual's different organs – heart, lungs, arteries, and so forth – participate in a single biological function (circulation of oxygenated blood) that contributes to the good of the system as a whole, and so are biologically united as parts of a whole individual, so too in coitus the male and the female participate in a single biological function performed by the couple as a unit. Coitus establishes a real biological union with respect to this function, although it is, of course, a limited biological union inasmuch as for various other functions (e.g., respiration, digestion, locomotion) the male and female remain fully distinct.

The human body is part of the personal reality of the human being and not an extrinsic instrument of the conscious and desiring aspect of the self. Human persons are not just spiritual subjects, or sets of experiences, or bundles of thoughts, memories, and feelings, that inhabit or supervene upon bodies; they are bodily beings, albeit of a special kind, namely, rational (including the capacity for deliberate choice) animal organisms. So, the biological unity just described can be a truly personal unity and a part (indeed, the biological foundation and matrix) of the comprehensive, multileveled (biological, emotional, volitional) union that marriage distinctively is. When a man and woman make a commitment to each other to share their lives on all levels of their being in the type of community that would be fulfilled by conceiving and rearing children together, then the biological unity realized in sexual intercourse is the actualization of that community we know as marriage.

This point is implicit in the traditional teaching, both in secular and ecclesiastical law, that the first act of sexual intercourse consummates marriage. Because the marital communion is bodily as well as emotional and spiritual, it is not fully established or completed until the spouses have become one at the biological level ("one flesh"). Before that, they are married in the sense of having the core of the marital union – the set of rights and duties toward one another to do what they reasonably can do to complete and build up the bodily, emotional, and spiritual union to which they have consented – but their union becomes completed in the specifically marital way only with bodily-sexual union. Subsequent acts of sexual intercourse, then, renew and embody their multileveled marital union. Thus, the sexual union of the spouses is the bodily component proportionate to, indeed, it is part of, the multileveled personal community to which they have consented in marrying.

Nor can sexual acts build up a personal communion simply as exchanges of gifts of pleasure. A community or friendship is a unity constituted by common pursuit of genuine goods such as health, knowledge, and the development and appreciation of worthwhile skills. Ordinary (or generic) friendships are constituted by sharing in, or common pursuit of, several goods (conversation, play,[5] etc.). Other types of communities, such as scholarly or sports communities, are actualized by cooperative pursuit of basic goods specific to them. But, as we indicated in Chapter 2, whether pleasure is a genuine good depends on that in which one takes pleasure. If pleasure were in itself a good, then we would have to say that, as much as we abhor the Nazi atrocities, and as devoutly as we wish they had never committed them, they were less bad than they would have been had the Nazis gotten less pleasure from them than they actually got. So, plainly, pleasure is not in itself a good. In general, pleasure is a genuine good only if it is an aspect of a condition or activity that is already genuinely a part of human well-being and fulfillment, and this point is also true of sexual pleasure. Hence sexual pleasure by itself does not constitute a fitting gift. To be a genuine good, it must be part of a sexual act that already realizes a genuine good. Since engaging in pleasure apart from participation in a real good by oneself is not truly humanly fulfilling, then (however elevated one's motives may be) giving this experience, or enabling

[5] As an intrinsic good, to be sure, play provides a basic reason for action. However, the good of play should not be equated with doing whatever one pleases. That would collapse play as a *reason* into a nonrational motive. Play, precisely as a rational motive, gives one reason to pursue more or less complex, frequently rule-based, activities (such as chess or football). It does not provide a reason to do whatever one wants to do precisely because one believes that pleasure is to be obtained.

someone else to have this experience, does not constitute a true gift. Hence the common good pursued together by a couple expressing or actualizing their personal union cannot be just sexual pleasure. In truly marital acts, the genuine, common good is their bodily, organic unity, as a noninstrumental aspect and the biological basis of the overall (multileveled) reality of their marriage. The only type of community a procreative-type act can actualize is a procreative-type community, that is, marriage.

Procreation as the Fruition of Marriage

The marital unity of the spouses – bodily, emotional, and spiritual – is extended and naturally fulfilled by conceiving and rearing children together. Their conceiving and bringing up children together fulfills the spouses precisely as a union of complementary (male and female) persons. So the cooperative rearing of their children does not establish a new type of relationship; rather, this activity deepens and naturally fulfills the relationship that they established precisely in marrying. Moreover, the child is the concrete fruit and expression of their marital commitment and their love for each other. Each child born of the marriage is the union of the spouses made concrete and prolonged in time.

Many deny that marriage is intrinsically oriented to procreation because they assume that the only way that it could be is as a mere means in relation to an extrinsic end. Because that is obviously false, they infer that marriage must really be only about love, not about procreation. Marriage, however, is centrally about *both* love *and* procreation: it is about the kind of love that can be expressed by two lovers uniting (becoming one) not only emotionally but also physically in the kind of union that would be unfolded and prolonged by becoming family. This union has its distinctive norms and basic structure because of its orientation to procreation and the education of children, but it is good in itself and so remains a true marital union even if it does not reach that fruition.

There are different kinds of love – but a love that can be expressed and lived out in a union that is bodily, emotional, and spiritual, and finds its fruition in procreation and the education of children together, is a distinctive type of love, namely, *marital* love (in other words, *conjugal* love). Indeed, *romantic* or *erotic* love is characterized by including a desire or longing for a bodily, sexual union – romantic or erotic love longs for a union with the beloved on all levels of one's being. But in fact that type of union *is* marriage. Hence the assumption that marriage must be either a mere means to procreation (and so actual procreation in each case must be at least possible) or, in its essence, without any intrinsic link to procreation is unsound. The union of the spouses is both intrinsically good (and so not a mere means) and, at the same time, intrinsically oriented to having and rearing children as its fruition.

Of course, a man and a woman might still choose to perform sexual intercourse as a mere means to conceiving a child or view their marriage as a mere means to procreation. But spouses should not regard their marital acts, or their marriage, in that way. To do so would be to treat their sexuality (their bodies-as-sexual) as mere instruments for the production of an extrinsic effect. And this, in turn, would treat children as mere products that are provided for someone else's benefit – either the parents' benefit, society's, or that of other interested parties. This denigrates children, since products derive their meaning and value from their producers. Since neither the sexuality of the spouses nor children themselves should be treated as a mere means, both the sexual act and the marital relationship as a whole should be valued for their own sakes, and procreation, the coming to be of children, should be recognized as a *gift* that supervenes on the embodiment of the spouses' marital love, not a *product* of the spouses' efficient activity.[6]

---

[6] Of course, it is possible to produce children in a laboratory, but this productive act is distinct from the act by which spouses become one. Moreover, this kind of act – artificial reproduction – is morally problematic, for the child, a distinct human person, is treated as if she were a mere product. She may be loved for her own sake after she comes to be, but she comes to be as related to her parents in the first moment of her existence as a product is related to a producer. Sadly, the widespread acceptance, and even celebration, of in vitro fertilization contributes to the commodification of children. See, e.g., Elizabeth

Thus, a central reason why marriage is a unique type of community is that having children – the fruition of this community – cannot properly be a goal of marriage in the same way purposes or goals can properly be for most other communities. As a form of human relationship, marriage is indeed intrinsically oriented to procreation – but as fruit of that union, as a gift that supervenes upon it, not as a goal the attainment of which must be possible for the relationship to make sense and be valuable.

So, marriage is a unique relationship, both like and unlike other relationships in different respects. Marriage is *like* ordinary friendships (and *unlike* a mere contractual relationship) in that it is good in itself and the members of this relationship care for each other for the sake of each other. It is *unlike* ordinary friendships (and *like* a contractual relationship) in that marriage requires explicit consent and has a definite structure. Marriage requires a definite structure and stability principally because of its orientation to having and rearing children, and so it must be a sharing of lives, and a long-term interpersonal community valued for its own sake, lest children be viewed as mere products. And because it requires stability, it can begin only with explicit, mutual, and usually public consent.

Between a Man and a Woman

From these points it is clear why marriage is the union of sexually complementary persons, that is, why marriage can only be between a man and a woman. Whatever the intensity of their emotional bond, same-sex partners cannot marry, simply because they cannot form together the kind of union marriage is. Marriage actualizes a distinctive potential in a man and a woman – the

Marquardt, *My Daddy's Name Is Donor: A New Study of Young Adults Conceived through Sperm Donation*, http://www.familyscholars.org/assets/Donor_FINAL.pdf; Leon Kass, "The Meaning of Life – in the Laboratory," *Public Interest* 146 (2002): 38–73, http://www.aei.org/article/society-and-culture/the-meaning-of-life--in-the-laboratory/; Alexander Pruss, *One Body: An Essay in Christian Sexual Ethics* (Notre Dame, IN: University of Notre Dame Press, 2013), 398–415.

potential to complete each other as complementary persons and form a unified couple, per se suited to be fulfilled further in cooperatively procreating and educating offspring of their union (even if per accidens that cannot happen). Hence, in order to marry, a couple must be able, in principle, to form a real organic union – not just an emotional and spiritual union – and form the kind of communion that would be naturally fulfilled by having and rearing children together. Same-sex partners cannot do either of these things. First, the sexual acts that persons of the same sex can perform on each other do not make them organically one and so cannot establish the bodily foundation for the multileveled union that marriage is. A mere geometrical "union" – say, sticking one's finger in a person's ear – does not unite the persons organically; a man and a woman in sexual intercourse, by contrast, become the single subject of a biological function. Second, same-sex partners cannot form the kind of union that would be fulfilled by having and rearing children together. Of course, same-sex partners can form sexual arrangements (not real organic unions), and can also cooperate in child rearing (as can other couples or other groups), but the one relationship is distinct and not inherently linked to the other.

Any couple who lacks the capacity, at least in radical form, to fulfill either of the conditions just mentioned cannot form a marriage. Just as couples who are too young to consent, or couples composed of individuals already married to other people, cannot marry, so same-sex couples cannot marry – since they are incapable of fulfilling either of those conditions. Thus, neither twelve-year-olds nor those who are already married can actually marry, because they are unable to form the kind of union marriage is; likewise, it is not mere prejudice or bigotry to deny that same-sex partners can actually form a marriage.[7]

---

[7] The impediment (inability to form marriage) is a defect of consent. A consent to form a union or relationship that is not a one-flesh union (i.e., founded in the biological union realized in sexual intercourse) and is not oriented to procreation (of the kind that would be fulfilled by procreation) is not a consent to *marriage.*

It might be objected that a same-sex pair might cohabit, regularly have sex together, and also adopt children and raise these children together. Why not call this a marriage and say that it is a community that has enlarged into family? Obviously, in such arrangements, there can be an intense emotional affection, and a genuine friendship, and there can be friendships and emotional bonds, of a different type, of those persons to the children. But these are distinct relationships not intelligibly connected to one another. And none of them is marriage. By contrast, in a marriage, the bodily union of spouses is part of the single union that unfolds into, and is fulfilled by, becoming family. The community we have identified as *marriage* is oriented toward the (multileveled) union of the spouses and toward procreation as two aspects of a single good. That distinguishes this community from others in an essential manner. That is, it distinguishes marriage from other communities on the basis of its specific nature and purpose. So, marriage is distinct from other communities essentially, not just incidentally (as is the case, for example, with communities distinguished on the basis of age, height, or ethnicity). Indeed, the orientation of the man and the woman toward children shapes their whole relationship.

Infertile Married Couples

We can now return to the argument (advanced by Chief Justice Marshall, Judge Walker, and others) to support the claim that marriage cannot be intrinsically related to procreation – on the ground that infertile, opposite-sex couples can get married. It should be clear by now how weak this argument is. The basic argument – as we saw previously, articulated by Marshall and Walker – is, *If marriage were intrinsically oriented to procreation, then couples who cannot procreate (the sterile or elderly) could not be married; but they can be married; therefore, etc.* But no reason is ever given why one should think that the first premise (the if-then proposition) is true. In fact, there are numerous reasons why this proposition could be false. And there is only one reason it could be true, namely, if marriage were – either as a community or as an institution – merely instrumental in relation to procreation, a relationship created simply as a means toward an extrinsic goal.

But plainly, as we have shown earlier, it is not. The comprehensive, multileveled union of husband and wife is both intrinsically good and the kind of relationship that would be naturally fulfilled by enlarging into family. Because marriage, thus understood, is good in itself, and not a mere means, men and women can marry even if they cannot, for any number of reasons, have children. To be genuinely married, a couple need not actually procreate, or even have within themselves all of the conditions prerequisite to actually procreating. For example, men or women with problems producing sex cells, or very elderly couples, can still marry. But in order to marry, a couple – any couple – must commit themselves to the type of personal union that would be fulfilled by bearing and raising children together and to the conduct by which they become biologically one, conduct that, with the addition of conditions extrinsic to that conduct, results in procreation. These two conditions together constitute the beginning of a marriage and are necessary for a consummated marriage.[8] But it is easy to see that infertile opposite-sex couples *can* form a true marital union. They are able to fulfill the two essential conditions just mentioned for marrying. First, infertile opposite-sex couples can form a biological union – they can mate (i.e., they can perform the kind of act that results in procreation when conditions extrinsic to their conduct obtain).[9] Second, infertile

[8] A couple might marry in a situation where having intercourse just after the ceremony is not possible or reasonable – for example, if they know they would likely conceive but have concluded that they should wait to have children or if they must live in different cities for a time after the ceremony. Yet genuine marital consent always includes a willingness to become bodily one with one's spouse. That conditional intention suffices for marital consent. Such conditional intention was part of the marital consent of Mary and Joseph, the parents of Jesus of Nazareth, to each other, even though – as Catholics believe – they had good reasons to abstain from intercourse.

[9] Mutual marital commitment is more than a contract, but not less. That is, the marital consent that initiates marriage includes a promise or commitment to do things that form a certain kind of union. The mutual promises create a moral

opposite-sex couples can form a bodily, emotional, and spiritual union of precisely the sort that would be naturally fulfilled by procreation and the rearing of children together – even though in their case that fulfillment is not reached.[10]

Not a Mere Construct

As we mentioned at the beginning of this chapter, one idea of marriage is that it lacks an objective structure, that its terms, norms, and content are up to societal or individual choice. We have already taken some care to emphasize that the idea of marriage set out here is not an arbitrary definition. Communities are of different kinds according to their orientation toward distinct types of goods or objectives or their pursuit of them in fundamentally different ways (e.g., one as an end and the other as a means). Thus, a study club is distinct in kind from a basketball team, even if some of the members (or even all the members) in the two groups overlap. What we have described as marriage has a single purpose or common good, even though that purpose has two interconnected aspects; thus marriage is a distinctive and single type of community. Its two aspects – the bodily, emotional, and spiritual union of the spouses and their conceiving and rearing children – are intelligibly related: the one

bond – a set of rights and obligations to each other – and initiate a multileveled community. The marital bond is the minimum part of marriage – what exists even if the spouses are emotionally estranged and even live in different cities. But this marital bond must exist if the community built on it exists as a genuine marriage. So if the marital consent – the mutual promises that give rise to the mutual rights and obligations – is not valid, then the marriage is null. What one promises in consenting to marriage is *voluntary conduct*, that is, to perform acts that will develop a marital communion. If one is radically incapable – incapable in principle – of performing such acts, then the agreement is invalid or null. That is why antecedent (i.e., existing before the marriage), radical inability to have sexual intercourse (inability in principle) is contrary to marital consent and so is an impediment to marriage, whereas radical inability to conceive a child – since conceiving a child is not directly voluntary conduct – is not an impediment.

[10] Further objections regarding the sexual acts of infertile couples are considered in the third section of Chapter 4.

(conceiving and rearing children) is simply the unfolding of the other (the initial union between the spouses). So, when John and Mary join in marriage, they begin their marital union. When they have children, they do not begin a new community; rather, the community they already have is enlarged, unfolds, and becomes a family. Their unity – the very unity for which they longed when they made their marital commitment – is extended in time and embodied in their children and their cooperatively rearing them.

This is quite different from couples who cohabit. They may cohabit and have sex on a regular basis for years but then at some point decide to get married, and so they have a ceremony in which they declare publicly a mutual, firm consent and have now formed a community that would be fulfilled by having and rearing children. When they do so, they have now formed a new type of community; they are now married, whereas before they were not. Conversely, a group of religious sisters may have an alliance dedicated to raising children, that is, an orphanage. This alliance is quite different from a marriage. Marriage is the kind of community defined by its purpose: forming a comprehensive, complementary union of the kind that is naturally fulfilled by enlarging into family.

Moreover, marriage is a distinct basic human good, and as such it has an objective structure (though also of course some flexibility to adjust for different personalities and circumstances). The following considerations provide support for this point. As we saw in Chapter 2, when we make choices, we choose to do something, or not to do something, *for a reason*, and the reason is a benefit or good we aim to achieve. Some goods are instrumental, but there must be some goods that we understand as good for their own sake. These *basic* goods are ultimate reasons for action. One might choose, for example, to take a medicine or to exercise: in each of these cases, one chooses to perform an action for the sake of becoming healthy or maintaining health. Health is a basic, noninstrumental good that, when grasped and understood to be attainable, is a reason for action – a reason to do something rather than nothing, and a reason to do this rather than that. Similarly, one might choose to go to a library in order to learn (here the good one seeks is knowledge), choose to visit a friend's house to play chess and build or maintain a friendship (the goods of play or skillful performance and friendship), and so on. The basic human goods, the basic reasons for action, are constitutive aspects of human flourishing, each of them distinct and irreducible: for example, being healthy does not as such realize the good of knowledge; play and skillful performance do not as such instantiate the good of health (though vigorous play may help cause or maintain health).

Since human beings are complex and can enter into personal relationships with others, there are many basic human goods, many distinctive and irreducible aspects of human well-being and fulfillment. Among the basic human goods, we include life and health, play or skillful performance, knowledge of truth, critical aesthetic appreciation, and various basic human goods that consist in harmonies, such as harmony with other human persons (friendship and society), harmony among conscience, choices and actions (self-integration or inner harmony), and harmony of ourselves with what we believe to be the greater-than-human source or sources of meaning and value (religion).

It is clear that marriage is also a distinctive, basic human good. It is an intelligible good that can provide a reason for action: one might choose to enter the communion of marriage for its own sake, and for the sake of the reality of the marital communion, not just out of erotic desire or fear, for example. Then, too, marriage actualizes a basic potentiality not actualized by the realization of or participation in any other good. Clearly, becoming a spouse and a husband-father or a wife-mother realizes a distinct aspect of the fulfillment of a human person. The distinctiveness of this basic human good is suggested by the fact that this fulfills the person precisely as male or female in a way not done by other basic goods. Moreover, although friendship between spouses is part of marriage, marriage is more than a specific type of friendship, for it centrally includes a biological union, and its culmination involves having children as well as the cooperative enterprise of raising them.

Like the other basic human goods, there is a great deal of flexibility in how this good will be realized. Still, because it is an irreducible way in which human beings are fulfilled, a distinct way in which their basic potential is actualized, it follows that the core of this good is grounded in the nature of human beings. In this respect, marriage is similar to health or to knowledge of truth. There is a variety of ways of pursuing and realizing the good of health, giving rise, for example, to diversity in cuisine, in ways of exercising, and, to a certain extent, in the art of medicine. Still, underlying this diversity is the basic good itself, a harmonious way of functioning by the human being as a sentient organism that has a definite structure, a structure that requires certain things (such as certain types of nutrients, vitamins, and minerals) and excludes actions that definitely impede or destroy that functioning. Similarly, marriage can be realized in various ways, but marriage is not a mere construct – whether individual or social. The core of marriage, the fundamental nature of marriage, is the actualization of a potentiality that is part of the nature of human persons. And marriage has a basic structure and contours that are not subject to modification by social or individual fiat.

Exclusivity

There is a difference between *what marriage is* (what makes it the specific kind of community it is) and its *properties* (characteristics that, although not part of what defines marriage, are not merely incidental but follow upon the kind of community it is, i.e., characteristics that the community should have, given its essential nature). A community is specifically defined by its purpose; a distinct purpose means a distinct community and a distinct type of relationship among members of that community. Thus, orientation to procreation and to bodily, emotional, and spiritual union – the two aspects of the one common good of marriage – distinguishes marriage from other types of community. But given this purpose, it follows as a logical consequence – or so we argue – that marriage ought to be between only one man and one woman and that it ought to be lifelong (until the death of the husband or wife).[11]

Although virtually every culture views marriage as a male-female union, in many cultures, polygamy (many spouses) is or has been accepted. However, in our judgment, an understanding of what marriage is shows that it should be between *one* man and *one* woman in an *exclusive* bond. Moreover, an understanding of what marriage is also shows – on the basis of ethical reasoning unaided by faith – that marriage includes a solemn pledge of permanence of commitment.

There are several reasons why marriage is by its nature exclusive. It can be seen first from the particular way marriage is related to the procreation and education of children. As we saw earlier, marriage is not a mere means in relation to procreation, but conceiving and rearing children is its intrinsic fruition. Now, the members of a community must be united with respect to those characteristics relevant to the common good of that community: they need not have the same roles, or perform the same behaviors in relation to the common good, but there must be a harmony and cooperative arrangement regarding those choices, actions,

---

[11] One cannot determine how many persons should be in a community or how long it should last until one first determines what the community is, what its fundamental, unifying purpose is. The number of members and the duration required by a community logically follow upon, rather than define, the community. So exclusivity and permanence are properties – logically speaking – of marriage rather than elements of what it is. And this point, it turns out, has practical importance. One can know what a community is, at least in a vague way – its basic purpose – but be mistaken about its properties, those attributes that should follow upon its nature. An error about the essential purpose of a community means one is not thinking of the same type of community at all, that one has failed to identify it or pick it out from other communities or relationships. However, given that unity and permanence are properties or logical consequences of what marriage is – attributes logically called for by the nature of marriage – it follows that one might consent to marriage and yet be ignorant or mistaken about its unity and permanence. And this means it is possible for someone to consent to marriage and yet be mistaken about the unity or permanence of marriage. In turn, this has practical implications in regard to what moral obligations people might have who are in such relationships, and what the state should do in regard to its regulations regarding marriage and the custody of children. See the fourth section of Chapter 5.

and attitudes relevant to that common good. The fulfillment to which marriage is intrinsically oriented is not just the conceiving and bearing of children but also bringing these children to maturity. But children mature in *all* aspects of being a human person: physically, emotionally, intellectually, ethically, culturally, religiously, and so on, that is, in every aspect of human life or flourishing.

And the spouses are committed to children not just as a part-time job but as the fruition of their bodily, emotional, and spiritual union. It follows that spouses should be united with respect to all aspects of their lives, not just in certain areas of their lives, as in ordinary friendships. Although they do not need to cooperate *directly* with respect to all of their projects – for example, read all of the same books or have all the same hobbies – they must in a real sense share with each other their whole lives, including their various projects, and so they should make a commitment to building a common life, committing their whole selves to each other. A consequence of this far-reaching commitment is that each is at all times related to his or her spouse as having a duty to care for and be responsible for him or her. Thus, marriage is *comprehensive*; it is a union of the spouses to each other with respect to all aspects of their lives.

That marriage should be comprehensive also follows from its sexual and romantic nature. In sexual intercourse, a man and a woman become organically one, a union that is naturally prolonged, if all goes well, by their conceiving children together, and cooperatively bringing them to full development or maturity. So, their bodily union of itself orients them to a dynamic unity extending into the indefinite future. Sexual intercourse is as complete a bodily union as two people can choose to bring about. So, if a man and a woman become one in body in sexual intercourse but *not* one in the other aspects of their selves, then they dissociate their bodies-as-sexual from the other aspects of the persons they are. If they unite their bodies but not their whole persons, they treat their bodies as mere extrinsic tools. So sexual intercourse actualizes a genuine good and is realized in a way that respects the sexual integrity of the other person only if it is a union of persons both bodily and personally, which is to say, a union of bodies (an organic union) that is an expression of, or part of, a comprehensive union of persons – a union of persons on all levels.[12] This comprehensive union is marriage.

This point can be seen also by focusing more specifically on romantic love. When a man falls in love with a woman, he longs to be with her, in fact, to be one with her – and eventually to be bodily and sexually one with her. And the same is true of the woman's desire when she falls in love with a man. Romantic love includes an appreciation of the other as a sexual being and a longing to be one with her in that respect. But the union for which romantic love longs is not *just* bodily and sexual. Romantic love longs for a union with the beloved on all levels of her being. Sexual union – uniting physically and biologically with the beloved – is the bodily aspect of the multileveled union that fulfills romantic love. But the bodily, or organic, union in sexual intercourse is brief. The full union to which romantic love is oriented must therefore be a union that extends beyond but includes this bodily union. The nonbodily aspects of the lovers' union will constitute an extension or prolongation of the bodily and personal union realized in sexual intercourse.[13] Thus, romantic love is oriented to a comprehensive union with the beloved, a union with the beloved in all aspects of her life.

Although this union encompasses all aspects of the spouses' lives, it is specifically marital in being a bodily and procreative-type union. The levels of their marital union that are not biological are shaped by their biological union and by its intrinsic orientation to the procreation and education of children (or by the fact that it would be fulfilled in that direction). When a man and a woman consent to share their lives in marriage, and consummate their union by becoming organically united, their entire union is

---

[12] Cf. Pruss, *One Body*, Chapter 6.

[13] Although a human person exists as a whole human being at each moment she exists, the person also develops her life in time, and this development is part of who she is. So, to be united with a person on all levels of her being requires being united with her throughout time, a union with her throughout her living her life, a union or sharing of lives.

continuous with that organic union – the nonbodily aspects of their union are in a way extensions of their organic union. Now, the organic union of the spouses is exclusive: a person can have sexual intercourse – become a single subject of a procreative-type act – with only one other person at a time. But the other aspects of the spouses' marital union are continuous with, and extensions of, that unity. The core of this union will be a responsibility – a belonging – to one's beloved. Thus, the specifically marital unity cannot be extended to other people. In this respect, marriage is unlike other friendships. The very same friendship – a union of wills regarding each other's well-being, shared memories, knowledge, and so forth – *is* extended and shared with other friends. Other friends can be added to one's friendship. However, other wives or husbands cannot be added to one's marriage without detracting from it precisely as the kind of bond it is.

Thus, if Jones marries and then attempts to marry again while the first Mrs. Jones is still alive, this second marriage would be outside of and competitive with, and therefore limiting the union of, his marriage to the first Mrs. Jones. In that case, although Mr. Jones could become "one flesh" (at different times) with two (or more) wives, he could not unite fully with either of them but would necessarily reserve or withhold part of his potentiality for uniting in a marital way from both. The unqualified commitment required of marriage either will not be made at all or will be severely diminished by the attempt to have a similar relationship with someone else. But marriage should be a union of one's whole self to one's spouse. So marriage should be between *one* man and *one* woman.

This point can be explained also in the following way. When John marries Sally, they become united bodily, emotionally, and spiritually; their union is not – or should not be – merely external. While remaining distinct persons, they form as it were a new unit. The spouses are complementary persons and form a procreative-type union – one that is characteristically (though not, of course, in every case) prolonged and deepened by their conceiving and rearing children together. Thus, John and Sally complete each other to become a new something, a marital union (uniting them on all levels of their being). After they are married, John is no longer ever just John by himself. From now on, he is John-married-to-Sally. And John-married-to-Sally added to Henrietta or Elizabeth cannot unite to make up a new marital union, that is, cannot form a marriage. Those who believe in polygamy believe that John can marry Henrietta and Elizabeth but do not think Henrietta and Elizabeth have been brought into the one marriage. Rather, they hold that John becomes married again, and then again, and so on. But that assumes that marriage does not result in a new reality – that John is not through and through changed when he becomes united with a spouse. And that assumption is false. If marriage is indeed a complete union of selves – a man and woman fully united to each other in all dimensions of their being – then polygamy is not an option. For a spouse of either sex to attempt marriage with another, or be open to an additional marriage with another, is to reduce marriage to a merely external union, not one involving a compete and self-transformative self-giving.

Moreover, polygamy is contrary to the mutuality of conjugal love and the equality of the spouses in the marital relationship. If one man has two or more wives (the most frequent type of polygamy), he is unable to give as much time and devotion to each wife as she is to him.[14] The one husband will have an essentially superior status to the many wives. So, wherever polygamy is practiced, it tends to lead to the demeaning of wives and women in general. (This lack of mutuality tends toward inequality, and so polyandry – one woman with many husbands – also leads to inequality, to the extent that the marriage is not reduced to an economic arrangement.)

Permanence

Marriage is quite unlike ordinary friendship, for ordinary friendships can be ended by mutual agreement, because the friends'

---

[14] And it will scarcely be possible to treat his wives equally, and so jealous rivalry will likely develop.

other interests and responsibilities move them in opposite directions or because circumstances cause them to drift apart.[15] Unlike ordinary friendships, marriage involves a commitment to share one's whole life. The spouses become as bodily united as people can choose to become. Their bodily union is extended or made an enduring and fully personal union by their commitment to unite on all levels of their being, and this bodily union is the root or embodiment of that dynamic unity between them. Thus, the spouses are united on all levels and in ways that cannot be undone without severe trauma. Now it is true that death itself divides the spouses. Because the distinctive form of their union and love is sexual and bodily, their marriage ends with one or both of them dying. However, deliberately to end marital unity can never be a simple undoing or return to a previous state. Rather, ending, or an attempt at ending, marital unity is analogous to the amputation of an important bodily organ. The breaking of marital unity necessarily is a severe trauma – not just to the spouses' feelings but to their integral well-being. So, if a person attempts to marry with the idea that he might later deliberately end the marriage (because, for example, it no longer suits him), then either that person is willing to harm his spouse in a fundamental way or he restricts their union and so his commitment is not to a sharing of his whole life – as it should be. But neither of those consequences is compatible with a genuine marital commitment. Hence the marital commitment is incompatible with a reservation that one might deliberately end it. Marriage calls for a lifelong commitment.

Moreover, the structure of marriage is shaped by its orientation toward conceiving and rearing children. Just as neither spouse can have sexual intercourse alone, and neither spouse can have children alone, so neither can adequately bring up children alone (though, of course, adverse circumstances, such as death or

---

[15] We think there might be a sense in which every friendship is meant to be lasting: one might never be justified in ceasing to care for, and being ready to help – subject to one's other responsibilities – a friend. But certainly, the cultivation or sustaining of an active friendship – active cooperation in pursuing substantive goods – can cease for reasons noted earlier.

abandonment, may require that). The union of the spouses is prolonged and fulfilled by conceiving and rearing children *together*. In turn, the child is fulfilled both by the relationship to her mother and by the relationship to her father – indeed, by the child's relationship to her mother and father as a marital *unit*. Thus, the child needs both her mother and her father. (Having both is not always possible, for example, a father may be called into armed service, may die, or may abandon his child. But a child has a natural need for – and a right to, if possible – the love and care of both her mother and her father.)[16] And so the spouses should be committed to being united at least for the duration of their child-rearing years (though, in truth, children are invested in their parents' marriages for the whole of their lives). Yet, as we have shown, it would be a mistake to treat the marital relationship as a mere means to conceiving and rearing children.[17] To do so

[16] The evidence that divorce almost always harms children in a family thus divided is overwhelming. It used to be thought that although children suffer terribly during and for some time after the divorce, they eventually fully recover from these bad effects. Sadly, there is compelling evidence against this assumption. See, e.g., Judith Wallerstein and Sandra Blakeslee, *The Unexpected Legacy of Divorce: A 25 Year Landmark Study* (New York: Hyperion, 2000). (Judith Wallerstein began this research decades before, to discover when children overcame the bad effects of divorce, but was forced to conclude that the bad effects on children persist into their adulthood.) Also see Linda J. Waite and Maggie Gallagher, *The Case for Marriage* (New York: Broadway Books, 2000), Chapter 9; *Marriage and the Public Good: Ten Principles*, signed by some seventy scholars (Princeton, NJ: Witherspoon Institute, 2008), http://protectmarriage.com/wp-content/uploads/2012/11/WI_Marriage.pdf. These studies provide compelling evidence of the importance of intact marriage for the well-being of children, as measured by numerous indices, including educational achievement, emotional health (rates of anxiety, depression, substance abuse, and suicide), familial and sexual development (sense of sexual identity, timing of onset of puberty, rates of teen and out-of-wedlock pregnancy, and rate of sexual abuse), and child and adult behavior (rates of aggression, attention-deficit disorder, delinquency, and incarceration).

[17] G. K. Chesterton made a similar point vividly: "The atmosphere of something safe and settled can only exist where people see it in the future as well as in the past. Children know exactly what is meant by having really come home; and the happier of them keep something of the feeling as they grow up. But they cannot keep the feeling for ten minutes, if there is an assumption that

would violate the good of the spouses and also treat the mature stage of children as a limited objective that can be attained by technically proficient means: that would violate the good of children as well as the good of the spouses. So, the interpersonal union of the spouses should not be contingent on getting the job done of raising the kids.

From this it follows that every aspect of the real fulfillment of the other spouse should be willed for his or her own sake – something that is also true in many ordinary friendships. But in addition, the spouses should be committed to sharing their lives in the manner that is suited to cooperatively rearing children, and so they should cooperate constantly with respect to the whole range of basic human goods. Their commitment can be called *total*, or *complete*, a commitment to a *total* sharing of their lives. But the temporal extension of the person is part of who he or she is. So, marriage should be a lifelong relationship. That is, in marrying, the man and the woman consent to form a procreative-type union, a union in which they pledge to each other the exclusive sharing of their procreative power. The fulfillment of this unity is actualized and prolonged in begetting and rearing children together. But this involves building a common life together, a common life that requires a commitment to lifelong union.

The commitment to be faithful to one's spouse – for better, for worse, in sickness and in health, until death do us part – is not a pledge to keep the same feelings that one has when the bride and groom exchange their consent and commitment. Rather, the consent to marry is a decision to enter a relationship that has an objective structure independent of the wills of the spouses. Men and women can decide to enter or not to enter the marriage relationship, but they cannot by their wills alter the

Papa is only waiting for Tommy's twenty-first birthday to carry the typist off to Trouville; or that the chauffeur actually has the car at the door, that Mrs. Brown may go off the moment Miss Brown has 'come out.'" Chesterton, *Brave New Family: G. K. Chesterton on Men and Women, Children, Sex, Divorce, Marriage, and the Family*, ed. Alvaro de Silva (San Francisco: Ignatius Press, 1990), 33–34.

fundamental kind of relationship marriage is. And marriage is, for the reasons explained earlier, the kind of relationship that should be permanent. There are, indeed, tragic situations where a wife or husband should *separate* from her or his spouse – for example, in situations of violence or abuse – but even then, in some (not all) of those cases, the innocent spouse may rightly conclude that he or she should remain open to reconciliation.

But can some marriages be dissolved or cease to be? Suppose a marriage has gone so badly – for any number of reasons – that love between the spouses and the ability to live together seem to have broken down so much that rehabilitation seems impossible. The spouses now lead separate lives. Are men and women in those marriages required to remain single? In our judgment, if one's commitment to marriage has not been made with a condition that negates that marriage's permanence, then, for the reasons given earlier, the obligation to remain committed to one's spouse does remain, even if that spouse has abandoned one and taken up with someone else.

Still, one cannot be bound by a commitment one does not make. So, if one commits to a union that one takes to be revocable, and so one's commitment itself is only conditional, then the marriage – in truth, an imperfect instance of marriage – *can* cease to be. So, some marriages – "marriages" in the broad sense – are dissoluble (these would not be sacramental marriages). Marriage (based on the kind of union it is) calls for an irrevocable and indissoluble commitment, but spouses do not always make such commitments. In those cases (where the commitment is conditional), it seems to us that they do have marriages, though not marriage in its fullness or focal sense – there is a failure to participate fully in the good of marriage. Lifelong marriage (even for spouses who do not believe marriage to be indissoluble) remains the ideal, and spouses should commit themselves to that.[18] Those

---

[18] As Catholics, we hold on the basis of faith that certain marriages are indissoluble – that is, not only that they ought not to be dissolved but that they *cannot* be dissolved. First, all sacramental marriages are indissoluble. Second – as a theological point, that is, a position reasoned to on the basis of revelation, but

couples who consent only to dissoluble marriage do not form
indissoluble unions[19] – and in some cases, for reasons of abuse
or other serious reasons, perhaps their marriages already have
been, or should be, dissolved. But generally speaking, marriage
ought not to be dissolved, and spouses have a strong duty to
remain true to their marital commitments. Marriage sometimes
requires great effort and patience. The commitment to anything
worthwhile and central to human well-being can involve hard
work and sometimes even pain and suffering. Men and women
who remain true to their marriage commitments, despite great
suffering, bear a great witness to the central and vital importance of marital fidelity. Like other great moral realities – such
as honesty and justice – fidelity to one's marriage commitment
may require great sacrifice.[20]

---

not as part of Catholic faith, that is, something that all Catholics must believe –
we hold also that some nonsacramental marriages could be indissoluble, that
is, if the parties to the marriage conceive of it as such and therefore consent to
marriage in the full sense. Christ taught that if a man puts away his wife and
marries another (meaning: attempts to marry another), he commits adultery,
and that marriage was meant to be this way – in effect, indissoluble – from
the beginning (see Matthew 5:32ff., 19:9ff.; Mark 10:11–12; Luke 16:18; and
1 Corinthians 7:10). This implies that not only Christian marriages but all
marriages where God himself has joined the spouses – and we can infer that
God joins the spouses in every marriage in the full sense – are indissoluble (see
Matthew 19:8 and Mark 10:5). So, marriages that God has joined – which
could include some marriages that are not sacramental – are such that man
cannot put them asunder, that is, are indissoluble.

[19] Note that Catholics do not believe that all marriages – in every sense of the
term "marriage" – are indissoluble. It is Catholic teaching that if a man or
woman in a nonsacramental marriage converts to the Christian faith, and the
spouse is opposed to him or her practicing the Christian religion, that marriage
might be dissoluble. The dissolution of such a marriage is referred to as the
Pauline privilege (see 1 Corinthians 7:10). Also, certain nonconsummated
marriages are dissoluble.

[20] Marriage is not indissoluble if either of the parties consenting to marriage
conceive of marriage as dissoluble. That is, if the bride or groom consents
only to a dissoluble relationship (i.e., conditionally intends to seek marriage
again, provided determinate or indeterminate circumstances obtain in the
future), then marriage in the full sense has not occurred. Since permanence
is a property of marriage, in the logical order, an attribute consequent to its
nature, then one can consent to marriage conceived of as dissoluble. Yet one
cannot be bound by an element in a contract (or covenant) the opposite of

In sum, the common good that defines marriage – and so its fundamental distinguishing nature – is the bodily, emotional, and spiritual unity that finds its fruition in bearing and rearing children together. The good toward which marriage is oriented is marriage itself, though the good of marriage has two tightly connected aspects, the unitive and the procreative.

Marriage is that type of community that is both a multileveled unity (a unity on all levels of the human person, including the bodily-sexual) and a community that would be fulfilled by having and rearing children together. There is an intrinsic link between these two aspects of the community; the multileveled (and intrinsically sexual) relationship is fulfilled by, and is not merely incidental to, the conceiving and rearing of children. Hence marriage is fundamentally distinct from a relationship of cohabitation combined with regular sex, and it is not merely an alliance formed to raise children. Rather, it is the union of a man and a woman, formed by their commitment to sharing their lives together, on all levels of their being – bodily-sexual as well as emotional and spiritual – in the kind of community that would be naturally fulfilled by begetting and rearing children together. This community is by its nature between a man and a woman and demands exclusivity and the sincere pledge of permanence.

what one has given one's consent to. So if one or both of the parties to marriage conceives of marriage as dissoluble, then their marriage is not indissoluble. On this point, see Germain Grisez, *The Way of the Lord Jesus: Vol. 2. Living a Christian Life* (Quincy, IL: Franciscan Press, 1993), 590–95. It remains that marriage *should* be permanent. As we see in Chapter 5, the fact that some marriages are dissoluble means that it is proper for the political community to allow and regulate divorces.

4

Sex Outside Marriage

Our inquiry centers on the nature of and relationship between sex and marriage. As our culture has become increasingly uncertain about what marriage is, serious questions have arisen about what makes sex valuable – what sex should be *for* – and how sex should be related to marriage. Is sex merely a pleasurable activity that people should enjoy whenever it is convenient, provided they avoid coercion, deception, disease, and undesired pregnancy? Or does sex have more inherent significance so that it should be reserved only for those with whom one has an ongoing, loving relationship, or even a marital bond? In this chapter, we examine the inherent significance of sexual acts and their relationship to marriage and procreation. In marital intercourse, husband and wife embody and express their multileveled union that is marriage. By choosing to embody their marital union in a sexual act, spouses give themselves to each other, for by this act, each intends the fulfillment of the other, and intends this act as part of the sharing of himself or herself with the other. Marital intercourse between spouses consummates or renews their marital union and so is itself a participation in – not a mere sign of or extrinsic means to – a basic human good, namely, the basic good of marriage itself.

Someone might claim that although marital intercourse does realize a distinctive good, nonmarital sex can realize other goods, even if on a lesser scale. Marital sex (it might be argued) might realize an exalted good, but it does not follow that every sexual act must realize this benefit in order to be morally right or permissible. Perhaps consensual sexual acts (between, say, strangers) done simply for the sake of pleasure, or sexual acts done to express or signify nonmarital, romantic relationships, are worthwhile and morally permissible, even though their benefits are less profound than the good of marriage.

In this chapter, we show that this proposal is mistaken. Our claim is that deliberately chosen nonmarital sexual acts not only fail to realize the good of marriage but inevitably violate that good. Nonmarital sexual acts involve, in one way or another, a depersonalization of the bodily, sexual person. People might choose to have sex either because it is pleasurable or to express their affection or romantic relationship. (There are, of course, many possible *ulterior* motives, such as money and revenge, but these two seem to be the immediate motives for having sex.) We discuss sexual acts done just for pleasure in the next section and sexual acts chosen to express a nonmarital sexual relationship in the following section. In the fourth section, we examine a common objection to our position, and in the fifth, we show that the idea that sexual acts can be morally justified simply as signs of affection or romantic attachment cannot account for the immorality of such practices as polyamory, incest, or even bestiality. (Of course, we acknowledge that this last point will make no difference to strict sexual liberationists who really don't think there is anything morally wrong with such practices.)

Nonmarital Sexual Acts Chosen Just for Pleasure

One might argue that, whereas marital sexual acts do have a profound meaning, other sexual acts can be just fun things to do without any significant implications. Such acts could be called casual sex or recreational sex. Why can't John and Sally, who are not married to each other, have sex simply for pleasure or for fun and reserve their *meaningful* sex for their future (or present?) spouses?

Such acts, however, violate the sexual integrity included in and required by sexual acts that realize a basic human good. Marriage and sexual acts that express marriage are possible only if the sexual acts and desires of the spouses are integrated with the commitments of the spouses to be one with each other – only if their sexual acts and desires are integrated into acts that unite the spouses to each other. This integrity or self-integration is principally rooted in the will and shaped by one's choices bearing on sex. For example, in order for Smith's sexual act with his wife really to actualize and enhance their personal communion, he must intend this act as an expression of their communion. If while having sex with his wife Smith wishes he were having sex with someone else and fantasizes about having sex with that other person, then he is not intending the realization or embodiment of his exclusive union with his wife but is merely using her – specifically, using her sexuality – to obtain a pleasant or enjoyable experience. His wish, or willingness, to have sex with someone else prevents him from giving himself – embodying his marital commitment – in his sexual act with his wife.

Or suppose Smith has sex with a woman other than his wife on Friday and then asks his wife to have sex with him on Saturday. Unless he has repented of his extramarital affair, he cannot intend this sexual act as an expression of his marital commitment; his willingness to have sex with other women prevents him from intending this act as embodying his exclusive, marital commitment, his commitment to share his whole life with his wife. A sexual act can embody or express a personal communion only if that embodiment is what is intended. Choices are not mere episodic events. When one chooses to do something, one has disposed one's will toward what one chooses, and that disposition remains as an aspect of oneself, an aspect of one's character. So a choice to have sex with someone other than one's wife remains – as a willingness or disposition – unless or until that choice is repented. If one has chosen adultery, that willingness to have sex with someone other than one's wife remains unless it is repented. But a willingness to have sex with someone to whom one is not married is incompatible with the exclusive giving of oneself that is involved in embodying one's marriage. Such a choice includes a distortion of one's regard for or attitude toward the good of marriage.

A similar point is true of sex *before* marriage. Suppose Jones has sex with someone before he is married. This willingness to have sex with someone to whom he is not married also remains as an aspect of himself unless he repents of it. And this willingness is incompatible with giving himself in marriage. By this type of choice, Jones renders himself unable (unless and until he reverses the choice) to intend a sex act as an embodiment of an exclusive gift of himself in marriage. This is so even if he intends to have sex with women to whom he is not married only during the time he is not married – say, he intends to be monogamous once he marries but promiscuous before that. For by choosing to have sex with someone to whom he is not married, he now approves of and consents to sex *as* nonmarital, as choiceworthy in itself apart from the context it might have within more encompassing marital union. Thus, unless he repents of that choice, what he regards as desirable in the sexual act is the same as what he could obtain from someone with whom he is not married.

Thus, for both married and unmarried persons, a willingness to have sex with someone other than one's spouse incapacitates one for the self-giving involved in the bodily completion (consummation) of marriage. This indicates that there is an intrinsic good consisting in the *integration* of one's sexual desires, choices, and acts with the other aspects of the person and with the genuine good that sexual acts can actualize. This need for integration applies both to sexual intercourse and to acts and desires that naturally prepare for or lead to sexual intercourse. Thus, the choice to have sex outside marriage includes in the content of that choice a diminishing of sexual integration, a disintegration. Choices that undo that integration are contrary to the good of marriage of which that integrity is an aspect. John Finnis has explained this point quite well. Speaking of the willingness to have sex outside marriage, Finnis says the following: "[Such willingness] disintegrates the intelligibility of one's marriage: one's sex acts, understood from the inside (so to speak) as the bodily carrying out of choices each made in a certain state of mind (will), no longer truly actualize and make possible authentic experience of one's *marriage*; they are unhinged from other aspects of the spouses' mutual marital commitment and project."[1] Such a choice *unhinges*, in one's intention and attitude, the bodily sexual act, on one hand, from the whole good of marriage, actual or possible, of which a sexual act would be a part, on the other hand. So, a nonmarital sexual act is contrary to the sexual integrity that is an aspect of the good of marriage and so is a choice that violates that good.

To understand this point more fully, especially as regards sexual acts chosen just for pleasure or enjoyment, we need to recall some points made in Chapter 2 about pleasure in general and apply them in particular to the issue of sexual pleasure. Pleasure in general is a conscious state or experience: it may be sensory (like the taste of an apple) or not directly sensory (like the experience of knowing one is admired or loved). Sexual pleasure, of course, usually includes a sensory component but also usually includes emotional gratification, such as a feeling of conquest, confirmation of one's sexual attractiveness, confirmation of one's masculinity or femininity, or (in marital intercourse where it is sought as an aspect of the marital good) the experience of bodily and personal unity. Now, when married couples choose to embody their marital union in sexual intercourse, they are usually motivated partly by the desire for sexual pleasure. However, they are pursuing sexual pleasure, not as a detached experience, but as an aspect of a genuinely fulfilling activity, namely, their sexual union as embodying their marriage. This is analogous to other types of choices: one might choose to eat eggs and toast for breakfast, for example, both because one is hungry (thus motivated by pleasure) and because one is aware, at least on some level, that eating breakfast is genuinely good for one; and in that case, one is pursuing a pleasurable activity, pleasure as an aspect of a genuinely fulfilling activity.

Such choices are morally good – in line with a love and respect for integral human good; and such pleasures are goods – worthy

---

John Finnis, "Sex and Marriage: Some Myths and Reasons," in *Human Rights and Common Good: Collected Essays* (New York: Oxford University Press, 2011), 3:379.

of pursuit – because they are aspects of genuinely fulfilling activities. Such pleasure is the experiential aspect of realizing a genuine good. However, in other cases, pleasure is the experiential aspect of an activity that is disordered or harmful, and then pleasure is *not* a good. Hence pleasure is not *by itself* a good. It is incorrect to say of the pleasure experienced by a sadist, for example, that, "Well, torturing a person is evil and he should not have tortured that child, but at least he got pleasure out of it; it would have been worse had he done it and not even gotten pleasure from it." And even if the pleasure is an aspect of a *neutral* activity – one that is neither fulfilling nor harmful (assuming that is possible) – then the pleasure is empty and indeed illusory, for one is treating *as* good and worthwhile something that is not so. So, pleasure is not just by itself a good; it is good only when and insofar as it is an aspect of a genuinely fulfilling activity. Whether a pleasure is a good at all depends on what one is taking pleasure in or the activity of which the pleasure is an aspect (by "good" here we do not mean *morally* good, but what is actually fulfilling, which includes goods other than moral integrity, goods such as knowledge and health). For a pleasure to be a genuine good, it must be connected to an *appropriate* object. If it is an aspect (the conscious experience) of a harmful or a worthless activity, then it is not a good.

The only genuine good that sexual activity can immediately actualize is bodily union as an aspect of a multileveled personal communion. Couples might, of course, have sex in order to engage in skilful performance or to perform strenuous activity to become more physically fit, but these would be ulterior ends. The sexual partners would directly intend the pleasure or experience attained in the sexual act, but not as an aspect of a genuinely fulfilling activity, and so the pleasure in such acts would be empty or meaningless. Thus, the choice to have sex just for pleasure involves adopting the attitude that a sexual act is of itself meaningless, though perhaps as capable of becoming meaningful by the imposition of intentions. But, as we have explained, sexual intercourse realizes an organic union, one that is suited to embodying a multileveled union oriented to procreating and rearing children together and building a common life. Sexual acts do have profound significance, independently of our choosing to bestow an extrinsic meaning upon them. And so, choices to have sex just for pleasure involve divorcing in one's intention the person as bodily and sexual from the whole person; they involve treating the bodily union realized in sexual intercourse (or acts that tend to lead to bodily union) as if it were not unitive, as if it were a mere tool for personal satisfaction. And so they involve a type of dualism in intention or attitude, a treating of the body (or the body-as-sexual) as if it were something extrinsic to, a mere tool of, the (nonbodily) personal subject. The sexual partners perform acts that unite their bodies, and thus unite the persons – since human persons are not separate entities from their bodies – or they perform acts that naturally lead to, and involve desires for, such bodily union; and yet this bodily union is treated as trivial, as subpersonal.[2]

The phenomenon of *obscenity* illustrates well the dualism and demeaning of sexuality involved in sexual acts and desires divorced from personal union. Obscenity involves sexual acts or pictures viewed from outside a first-person perspective, that is, viewed as separate from any pretensions of personal involvement and attachment with the persons being observed. The sexuality of those who are observed is used as a mere means for obtaining experiences for the viewers, and their sexuality is detached in each observer's intentions from the real being of the persons who are observed. Thus, Roger Scruton points out that the copulation of human beings in public strikes most people as obscene because such acts done in public are viewed from a point of view outside the first-person perspective of those engaged in it and thus as detached from any personal involvement. And so their acts and their bodies are reduced to mere means in relation to the pleasure obtained by the observers.[3]

---

[2] An argument similar to ours is set out by Mary Catherine Geach, "Lying with the Body," *The Monist* 91 (2008): 523–57; and Alexander Pruss, *One Body: An Essay in Christian Sexual Ethics* (Notre Dame, IN: University of Notre Dame Press, 2013), Chapters 6 and 8.

[3] Roger Scruton, *Sexual Desire: A Moral Philosophy of the Erotic* (New York: Free Press, 1986), 138–39.

Similarly, in the consumption of pornography, one deliberately obtains sexual pleasure from viewing a picture of a woman
(to consider the most frequent type) and takes sexual pleasure
in viewing, and perhaps fantasizing, acts of the most profound
intimacy with someone with whom one has no personal relationship at all. In viewing pornography, one reduces the sexuality of
those observed to mere means and has divorced, in one's regard
or intention, the sexuality of the woman from the other aspects of
her being as an integrated and whole person (even if the woman
used has consented to this use). Therefore, treating a person's
sexuality – the body-as-sexual, which is not other than the person herself – as a mere means in relation to obtaining pleasurable
experiences – as opposed to taking pleasure in genuinely fulfilling sexual acts – is to divorce in one's intentions the bodily (or
animal, including the other's sexual desire) from the personal.
Treating the sexual as a mere means to obtain a pleasurable feeling or experience involves a dis-integrity, a disharmony in one's
intention between the body-as-sexual and the body as a whole
human person.

It is precisely because we are aware, at least on some level, of
the importance of sexual integrity that we rightly regard sexual
acts as profound or as having a deep significance. This is why
sex requires mature consent, why rape is a grave violation, and
why we generally take much more care about whom we have sex
with than we do about whom we play tennis with. This is why
the cheating husband who protests to his wife that the sexual act
he had with his mistress was meaningless, though the sex he had
with her was meaningful and genuine, is proposing a radically
unsound argument. This is why men who have sex with children
are violating them, whereas parents teaching them how to swing
a bat (involving bodily cooperation) does not violate them.

The bodily sexual act itself has a profound significance that
other bodily acts do not have. In sexual intercourse, one becomes
fully united, organically one, with another person. It is the deep-
est bodily union one can choose to have with another person,
and it is the kind of bodily union that calls for union on all levels
of the person, a union extended into the indefinite future – and

other sexual acts derive a comparable profundity because of their connection to sexual intercourse. Thus, a sexual act is in truth far from trivial, and it involves a violation unless it is done with someone with whom it is appropriate to have such a union, that is, unless it is done with a person with whom one has the kind of personal union that such a sexual act can embody or be part of. Otherwise, there is a dissociation of the person as sexual from the whole person and a demeaning of that person's sexuality.

Thus, included in what is chosen in nonmarital sexual acts is dis-integration, a diminishing of sexual integrity. Indeed, in consenting to nonmarital sex, one adopts the attitude that the integral good of marriage is *incoherent*, an admixture of two things – like oil and water – unable to form a true unity. By choosing to use one's sexuality apart from a real marital communion, one adopts the attitude – both volitional and cognitive – that sex is a mere bodily act that may or may not have any profound significance, but if so, only from extrinsic intentions. This attitude is a standing denial of the real capacity of sexual acts to *be part of*, and *to embody*, the bodily-emotional-spiritual union, procreative in its fulfillment, of a man and a woman. Such a choice is a violation of the good of marriage and a distortion of one's view of marriage and of human life itself – since the body is viewed as "merely biological" and subpersonal. This helps to explain why the great moral teachers of humankind – from Plato to St. Augustine and from the Buddha to Gandhi – have treated sexual immorality not as a trivial matter but as a serious falling away from virtue.

Nonmarital Sexual Acts Chosen to Express Love or Affection

A couple who is not married may also choose to have sex, not just for pleasure, but for the purpose of promoting their romantic, personal relationship. It might be objected, then, that a sexual act might in some way foster or enhance a personal relationship – and be chosen for that reason – even though the couple are not married. And, whereas marital sex fosters marital union (the objection continues), sex chosen as a way of promoting a romantic (but nonmarital) relationship, or to express one's love or affection to someone with whom one is not married, can still promote a real human good and therefore, at least in some cases, be morally right.

There are three types of extramarital sexual acts done to promote a relationship or to express love or affection: sodomy, fornication, and adultery. We treated adultery in Chapter 3. In this section, we discuss the other two types and show how each violates the marital good.

Sodomy

By *sodomy*, here is meant (1) anal or oral intercourse between persons of the same sex or (2) anal or oral intercourse between persons of opposite sexes (even if married), if it is intended to bring about complete sexual satisfaction apart from coitus.

In a truly *marital* act, the spouses actualize a basic human good because their bodily union actualizes and enables the spouses to experience their marriage; indeed, it is an integral part of (and in a sense the very foundation of) their marriage as a multileveled union of persons. But in a sodomitical act (even between spouses), no organic (i.e., biological, and in that sense truly bodily) union is realized.

If Sally, for example, masturbates John to orgasm or orally stimulates him to orgasm, no biological unity has been effectuated. Likewise, if John and Steve engage in mutually sexually stimulating activities – manual, oral, or anal – these acts do not realize a biological union. In a sodomitical act, one person's inserting a bodily organ (sexual organ or finger) into another's orifice (mouth or anus) provides some spatial contact and juxtaposition, but the two do not become organically or biologically one, do not become a single subject of a unitary biological act, as occurs if a man and woman engage in an act of coitus. An organic union occurs when different material components participate in a single action, to which each is internally oriented, for the sake of the whole of which they are parts. For example, the heart, lungs, and arteries participate in a single action, to which each is internally oriented, for the sake of the whole body of which they are parts – and so we recognize them as parts (organs) of a single organism. In sexual intercourse, sexual parts of the male cooperate with sexual parts of the female in a single action – coitus – that is oriented to reproduction, which is the (biological) fulfillment of the couple as a unit. By contrast, when a surgeon puts her hand inside a patient's body, or a mother puts her finger inside her child's nose, no organic, functional union has been established, though there is overlap and contact.[4] Contact and overlap are not the same as an organic union.

It follows that sexual acts of this kind performed on each other do not actualize personal unions. Friendship, or personal communion, is a union of persons primarily with respect to their choices and acts of will. A friendship or personal communion is constituted when two or more people work together for common goods, not only for the sake of their own share in those goods, but for that of the other(s) as well, and thereby constitute themselves as one. This unity – that is, this disposition toward the fulfillment of each other for the other's own sake – *is* their friendship or community. Thus, people cultivate friendships by, for example, attending a movie together (sharing in the good of aesthetic experience), going jogging or to the gym together (the good of health), having conversations (the good of knowledge and perhaps play), or playing a game together (the goods of skillful performance and play).[5] But in sodomitical acts, no genuine common good is realized. So if the sodomitical act is not chosen simply to obtain pleasure, then it is chosen for the purpose of having the *experience of unity* but without sharing in a genuine common good. In that case the act is chosen only for the sake of having *the experience* of union, without its reality – and that is so even if the participants hope that it will foster

---

[4] See also Pruss, *One Body*, 96–102.
[5] Just as pleasure is good only if taken in some object that is already or independently a good, so people build up personal unity only by a unified pursuit or participation in some object that is independently a good. John Corvino's failure to address this point mars his exposition of and attempt to rebut our argument that nonmarital sexual acts are immoral, in *What's Wrong with Homosexuality?* (New York: Oxford University Press, 2013), 87–96.

their personal communion. But the choice to pursue the illusory experience of a bodily-personal communion, detached from a real union, introduces in one's regard for the good of sexual integrity – in other words, the good of marriage – a dis-integration, and so a distortion and diminishing of one's appreciation of that good.

It might be objected that sexual acts enhance personal relationships (serving the good of friendship) simply by being exchanges of pleasure. However, just as John and Sally's injecting each other with a euphoric drug does not build up their personal relationship,[6] simply giving each other sexual pleasure does not actualize or enhance their friendship. Again, to be a genuine good, pleasure must be an aspect of a genuinely fulfilling activity. Here, on the contrary, it is an empty pleasure. Thus, John and Sally's (or John and Steve's, or John and Sally and Steve's) providing each other pleasure is mutual gift giving only if the pleasure they experience is an aspect of something really fulfilling, and that is lacking in sodomitical acts.

Someone might object that providing pleasure to another does provide a genuine gift because there is a *need* for pleasure and satisfying a bodily need realizes a genuine good.[7] However, this objection implicitly confuses a desire with a need. It is true that a desire, particularly one for sex, for a particular kind of sex, or for sex with a particular person, may cause tension, and the release of that tension may have a calming effect on the person who had the desire. But it does not follow that the satisfaction of that desire is a good or satisfies a real need. For example, someone who strongly desires to have sex with Miss Smith – whom he knows only from pictures in a magazine – and from this desire has considerable tension and nervousness, will not

---

[6] Please note that we are not here asserting that nonmarital sex acts are the moral equivalent of drug using. Our point here is a narrow and analytical one designed to show that exchanges of pleasure are, just in themselves, not acts that embody or express the good of friendship or build up personal relationships.

[7] Andrew Koppelman, *The Gay Rights Question in Contemporary American Law* (Chicago: University of Chicago Press, 2002), 85. Gareth Moore, "Natural Sex: Germain Grisez, Sex, and Natural Law," in *Revival of Natural Law*, ed. Nigel Bigger and Rufus Black (Burlington, VT: Ashgate Press, 2001), 232.

actually receive the fulfillment of a genuine *need* if she agrees to
have sex with him in return for money.

Human beings find sexual genital stimulation and orgasm
pleasurable, and so acquiring it has the effect of release of tension. But the actual need is oriented to the pleasurable activity,
not just toward the pleasure. For example, hunger involves a tension, and eating – even if what is eaten is not genuinely good for
one – relieves that tension. But, understood more clearly, hunger
is a desire connected to a need and orientation to eating *food*
and being nourished. The object of the *need,* as opposed to the
object of a desire not rooted in a need, is eating a nourishing
substance – a genuinely fulfilling activity. A desire, just as such,
may be misdirected. And so even if a person took pleasure in eating Styrofoam or plastic, this would not show that eating these
substances answers to a genuine need.[8] Such desires would be
disorders in the basic orientation or natural desire (the actual
need) for real food.

The desire for sex is much more complicated than the desire
for food and involves one's capacity to relate to another in a
personal manner in a way that a desire for food does not. But the
two desires are similar in this respect: one should ask, in both
cases, what is the really fulfilling condition or activity to which
these desires are actually oriented? As the desire to eat plastic is
really a disordered desire for real food, so the desire for sexual
pleasure or for an experience isolated from bodily and personal
communion is a disordered desire for what sex offers that is really
fulfilling, the expression or embodiment of a real interpersonal –
indeed, marital – union. So, the fundamental need that is the
object of the desire for sex (or is connected to the desire for sex)
is real bodily-personal communion – in fact, marriage, to which
sexual acts can contribute – not merely the satisfaction of an
urge. Sexual pleasure by itself is not the genuine good realized
in a sexual act, and it cannot be the common good uniting two

---

[8] Please note that we are not asserting that engaging in nonmarital sexual conduct
is the moral equivalent of eating plastic or Styrofoam. Again, our point is a
narrow and analytical one, as the following paragraphs make clear.

(or more) persons in a sexual act, since pleasure is a genuine good only if it is an aspect of an activity or condition that is already intrinsically fulfilling.

One could also object that a nonmarital sexual act can realize a genuine good by being a *sign* of love, or at least a sign of some degree of affection for another. So, even though John and Sally, or John and Steve, do not become biologically one in their sodomitical acts, someone might argue that their acts express their love or affection for one another.

However, although it is true that marital acts *are* signs or symbols of personal union, they are in their immediate reality *much more* than symbols or gestures. The question is whether the reality that is more than symbolic – the act of sex itself – involves a violation of the marital good. Someone may have sex with another with the ulterior intention of signifying something. For example, an otherwise unwilling teenage girl may consent to have sex with her boyfriend to prove to him how much she cares, or a young woman may have sex with her boss to show her determination to succeed. Still, the immediate reality of the sexual act is not a mere sign or gesture. And so if there is not a real union of which the sexual act is a part – in other words, if the sexual act does not embody marital communion – then no genuine good is realized in the act, and the choice to pursue that illusory experience violates the marital good.

In sum, a sexual act can be a way of building up a personal communion only if it is sharing in a genuine good – that would be the common good of the participants' act. If their act has a common good, then it is an act in which the two share and therefore become one in jointly performing this act. In that case, their pleasurable experiences will be aspects of a real good. In the case of marital intercourse, spouses participate in the real good of marital bodily union. In marital intercourse, the man and the woman become organically one in an act of coitus, and this organic union consummates or renews their total marital communion: in this case, there is an identifiable, real good in which they share, namely, the act of consummating or renewing their marital union in their becoming organically (i.e., biologically) one. But in sodomitical acts chosen to enhance a personal relationship, no true common good is realized in the act, and so the participants in these acts are pursuing an illusory experience of a union not actualized in this act. Therefore such acts are not realizations of human goods, and they involve a choice that distorts their regard – intentional, affective, and cognitive – of the marital good.

Fornication

There must, then, be an organic unity if there is a common good in the sexual act. But this organic unity is an instance of a real human good only if it is an aspect of a real union of the persons. If they are biologically united but are not united in other aspects of their lives or selves, then they are choosing, not an instance of a genuine good, but the illusory experience of one. But suppose a man and woman have a friendship and perhaps are considering, or even planning, marriage in the future. Suppose they have sexual intercourse and intend their act not just as an experience of pleasure but (perhaps confusedly) as an embodiment of their personal but not-yet-marital communion. In this case, they really do become biologically one in the sexual act, and so their act might *seem* to be a sharing in a common good. They become biologically one, and they intend this union to be an actualization and experience of their personal communion, though this is not yet a marital communion. This type of act has traditionally been designated as "fornication." Could one argue that fornication can embody a deep, though nonmarital personal union and so could be morally right?

If sexual intercourse does embody a personal communion, it does not embody just some personal community or other or some nonspecific type of communion or friendship. If sexual intercourse does embody a personal communion, it embodies the type of personal communion that is fulfilled by the man and woman's sexual complementarity, that is, the type of personal communion in which sexual acts can, or would, produce their full effect. That is, the only type of personal union that reproductive-type acts can actualize and embody is a reproductive-type community. But if such a community does not exist (or does not yet exist) between the man and the woman, then there is no such community to actualize or embody, and their act is the pursuit of an illusory good.[9]

In sum, in loving marital intercourse, the spouses act in a fully integrated way. Each bodily person relates to the other precisely as a bodily person, because they complete each other and become physically and personally united. In nonmarital sexual acts, however, either the participants unite in a bodily way but not as actualizing a personal communion, or they do not really unite but use their sexual powers to pursue a mere illusory experience of a genuine good. It remains that such choices dis-integrate the bodily-emotional-spiritual good of marriage.

The Sterility Objection

We have argued that in loving marital acts, husband and wife become biologically one to actualize and express their marriage, and that sodomitical acts – whether between people of the same sex or of opposite sexes (even if engaged in affectionately) – do not constitute a biological union and thus do not embody a personal communion. It is often objected against this position that, if it were true, it would also follow that the sexual acts of infertile married couples cannot be marital.[10] This has been dubbed the "sterility objection." The argument is that if a couple

---

[9] As Germain Grisez expresses it, "the part of the good of marital communion which fornicators choose, bodily union, is not an intelligible good apart from the whole. Although bodily union provides an experience of intimacy, by itself it realizes only the natural capacity of a male individual and a female individual to mate. Sexual mating contributes to an intelligible good, which fulfills persons, only insofar as it is one element of the complete communion by which a man and a woman become, as it were, one person." Grisez, *The Way of the Lord Jesus: Vol. 2. Living a Christian Life* (Quincy, IL: Franciscan Press, 1993), 651. Of course, the "as it were" in Grisez's account is important, since (as he fully recognizes) personal *identities* do not merge in acts of bodily union. So there is no assertion here that the man and woman, having truly become one in a certain important sense, cease being separate individuals.

[10] Paul Weithman coined the term *sterility objection*, although he himself does not endorse it. See Weithman, "Natural Law, Morality and Sexual Complementarity," in *Sex, Preference, and Family, Essays on Laws and Nature*,

is incapable of conceiving a child in their acts of sexual congress
(e.g., an elderly married couple), then their sexual acts are related
to procreation in the same way that the sexual acts of same-sex
partners are related to procreation, that is, they are *not* related.
Since procreation is not possible, the point of their sexual acts
must be (it is argued) pleasure, or to express their friendship or
affection, or some other shared good.[11] If the coital intercourse
of infertile married couples can be marital – and no one denies
that it can be – it follows that sodomitical acts can be marital, and
marriage, therefore, need not require sexual complementarity.

However, there is a clear difference between sodomy and marital coitus, even where coitus cannot result in conception. No one
could have children by performing sodomitical acts. Yet, this is
not true of the *kind of act* performed by sterile married couples
when they engage in coitus. A man and woman who are not
temporarily or permanently infertile *could* procreate by doing
exactly what the infertile married couple do when they consummate or actualize their marital communion. The behavior is identical and the intention – the actualization of marriage considered
as a multileveled union founded upon organic bodily union –
can be identical as well. Thus, the difference between infertile
and fertile married couples is not a difference in *what they do or
in the act they perform*. There is no difference in their voluntary
conduct. Rather, it is a difference in an extrinsic condition that
affects what may result from what they do. So, the premise of the
objection is simply false: it is not true that what infertile married
couples do when they unite biologically in coitus is the same act
or the same kind of act that is performed by partners (whether
opposite sex or same sex, and, if opposite sex, whether married
to each other or not) when they engage in sodomy.

Both fertile and infertile married couples perform marital acts
by realizing an organic, or biological, union in acts that fulfill

---

ed. David Estlund and Martha Nussbaum, 227–48 (New York: Oxford University Press, 1997).
[11] Stephen Macedo, "Homosexuality and the Conservative Mind," *Georgetown
Law Journal* 84 (1995): 278. Also see Koppelman, *Gay Rights Question*.

the behavioral conditions of procreation. The fact that the non-behavioral conditions of procreation happen to obtain or not obtain does not affect or alter what they do. To fail to see this is to fail to understand the intelligibility of the historic conjugal conception of marriage as a "one-flesh union." The object of the marital act in this instance – the union of spouses as bodily persons, as part of a multileveled sharing of life that would be fulfilled by the generating and rearing of children together – is precisely the same. In fulfilling procreation's behavioral conditions, married couples realize organic unity (thus consummating or actualizing the intrinsic good of their marriage) whether the nonbehavioral conditions of procreation obtain or not.

Someone might attempt to resist the force of this point by claiming that males and females become organically one only if they actually conceive a child. But it can easily be shown that this line of objection fails. Suppose a male and a female engage in coitus early one evening but something happens to the female later that prevents a conception from occurring that otherwise would have occurred. This event cannot retroactively change the nature of the action they performed together. The act that they performed together really did fulfill the behavioral conditions of procreation, and so really did unite them organically as a single subject of a biological action. By uniting sexually, they performed the first step in the reproductive process, even though conditions extrinsic to their voluntary behavior prevented its completion. Remember that the conditions for a successful conception are not all within the scope of their behavior. Whether coitus results in conception depends on conditions extrinsic to the act itself. But whether their action does unite them organically cannot depend on something wholly extrinsic to that action. So, in *every* act of coitus, the male and the female become organically one (even if, as in adultery, their act is intrinsically nonmarital).

If conception *does* occur, that may be hours or even days later; and whether they *now* become one cannot depend on events that occur only later. Hence one cannot say that the male and the female unite organically only in those acts of coitus that actually result in conception. In coitus itself – whatever may happen *after* coitus – the male and the female become biologically united. Their reproductive organs are actualized, as internally designed, to be a (now) unitary subject of a single act. So, this biological difference means that in coitus – as opposed to sodomy (whether between same-sex or opposite-sex partners), mutual masturbation, and so on – the male and the female genuinely (albeit in a limited sense, since identities do not merge) become "one flesh," a biological unit.

In a recent article,[12] Koppelman poses the following objection to our position. He contends that if one knows[13] that a process cannot be completed, then one's action cannot take its meaning from facilitating that process. For example, according to Koppelman, a surgeon can try to save the life of a severely injured or ill patient, that is, perform a "medical-type act" (analogous, he supposes, to a procreative-type act or, in Anscombe's words, "an act of the generative kind") – only if the surgeon knows (or believes) there is some chance that the surgery will succeed. In other words, if the end of the medical act (restoration of some healthy functioning) were known to be impossible, then the surgeon's act could not be classified as a medical-type act.

However, the key premise here – that an action that is known to be incapable of attaining an end cannot be oriented to that end – is simply false. It is true that an act cannot be *intentionally* (i.e., by conscious will) oriented toward an end if one knows that the end is impossible of attainment. But our claim is that the marital acts of infertile couples are *biologically*, not *intentionally*, oriented to procreation – they are acts of mating. Koppelman has either confused the two or simply ignored biological orientation. This point is confirmed by the fact that his analogies, without exception, refer to actions that receive their unity from conscious intention; none refers to an action that has a biological orientation and unity. Sherif Girgis rightly points

---

[12] Andrew Koppelman, "Careful with That Gun: A Reply to Lee, George, Geach, and Wax," Northwestern Public Law Research Paper 10-06, http://papers .ssrn.com/sol3/papers.cfm?abstract_id=1544478.

[13] Koppelman uses the word "knows" but perhaps should have said "believes." Nothing depends on that distinction here.

out (in a brief reply to Koppelman on the *Mirror of Justice* blog) that the processes in Koppelman's analogies are artificial actions and have their functions by human choice; none refers to natural actions, such as digestion, blood circulation, or respiration, which have their functions from nature.[14]

An action that is part of a larger process that is biologically oriented toward an end can receive its meaning (and so be a certain kind of action) because of its place within this larger biological process, and even if extrinsic circumstances make the end unattainable at this point. This is clear in virtually all complex biological processes, such as respiration, metabolism, growth, and neural activities. Coitus is an action that has a biological identity as part of the reproductive process. As a biological matter, coitus is plainly oriented to reproduction. Moreover, coitus remains coitus, that is, it remains a naturally unified biological action that fulfills the behavioral conditions of reproduction and is thus biologically oriented to reproduction, even if the nonbehavioral conditions of reproduction do not obtain.

Most biological processes are complex, and a first part of the biological process can remain oriented to the end of the process (and fully intelligible only as such), even if some condition prevents the completion of the process. This is why, for example, the acts of eating food, and of digestion, the first two parts of the larger process of *metabolism*, are still biologically oriented toward obtaining nutrients or energy from external substances for the maintenance of internal vital processes. Similarly, the act of breathing is only part of the more complex process of respiration. In modern intensive care units, machines (ventilators) sometimes do the breathing for a person, while the rest of the respiratory process is completed by the patient himself or herself. Thus, eating is not the same as metabolism; breathing is not the same as respiration. In the same way, copulating or mating

[14] Sherif Girgis, "On Guns and Knives, Generative (or Reproductive-Type) Acts," *Mirror of Justice Blog*, March 29, 2010, http://mirrorofjustice.blogs.com/mirrorofjustice/2010/03/sherif-girgis-on-guns-and-knives-sexual-organs-and-generative-or-reproductivetype-acts.html.

(coitus) is not the same as reproducing, though it receives its biological unity from its being a part of that larger process and thus being biologically oriented to procreation. Coitus is an action that has a biological identity as part of the reproductive process. That is how biology, considered as a scientific discipline, makes sense of it as a phenomenon.

We usually have direct voluntary control over only some parts of a biological process (e.g., eating, with respect to metabolism; or coitus, with respect to reproduction). In these cases, the behavior over which we have direct voluntary control depends for its biological success on conditions outside our direct control. With respect to those processes, *what we do* (and the object of our choice) has a discrete biological identity, but this identity is derived from its being part of a larger process. Thus, we can choose to eat but not to perform internal digestion and absorption of nutrients; we can choose to take a breath but not to complete the respiration process that ends with the absorption of oxygen by blood cells. All these actions, however, receive their identity from being oriented to ends of larger processes – metabolism and respiration. Similarly, we can choose to have coitus, that is, to mate, but not (in a sexual act) directly to conceive. But, in addition, we can choose to have coitus only together with someone of the opposite sex. Like eating or taking a breath, mating receives its identity and unity from its orientation to the end or goal of a larger biological process – which (in the normal course of things) we cannot directly choose – namely, to conceive or procreate. (At most, we can choose only to fulfill the behavioral conditions of procreation and to try to fulfill them at a time when the nonbehavioral conditions obtain.)

Thus Koppelman's arguments by analogy fail: he ignores a crucial dissimilarity between the cases he cites (surgery, shooting an unloaded gun, etc.), on one hand, and coitus or sexual intercourse, on the other. The former have their unity by conscious intention; the latter has its identity by nature or biology. Although he is quite right that it makes no sense to speak of surgery on a corpse as a "medical-type act," he fails to see that this is simply because medical acts receive their unity and meaning from the human *intention* of restoring healthy functioning. And this also is why shooting a gun known to be unloaded at someone is not homicide or a homicidal-type act: homicide receives its unity from a conscious intention.[15]

This difference between procreative-type acts and other sexual acts is morally significant, because marriage is the *human community* oriented to, and proportionate to (i.e., suited to,

---

[15] Someone might object that the biological identity of an act is irrelevant to its moral identity. Are we not falsely identifying the moral and biological realms? How can the identity of a human choice depend so closely on the biological identity of a material action? However, we have not identified the moral act (the act of choice) with the biological act. The moral act need not have the same structure as the biological act. For example, a man might choose to perform the behavior involved in coitus – that is, to mate – without choosing to become one with his female sexual partner: he might be choosing this behavior merely as pleasure-producing behavior, or as a way of asserting power, and accept as a side effect that this involves biological unity. But the important point here is that one cannot effectively choose to become fully united with one's spouse in the truly marital way – where bodily union actualizes and is part of the multileveled sharing of life that is marriage – unless one unites with him or her biologically. Coitus *makes it possible* for a man and a woman who want to consummate or actualize their marriage – considered not as a mere emotional bond but as a comprehensive sharing of life at all levels of the being of human persons, including the bodily or biological – to choose to do so. The biological identity of the action does not necessitate what will be the content of the choice. By contrast, the biological identity of the action *makes it possible* for one to choose to embody in this act the multileveled, marital union.

It makes a difference whether what one offers one's wife to drink is a poison or a tonic, whether what one dissects is a human being or a corpse. In the same way, it makes a difference whether the action one chooses to perform unites one biologically with one's spouse or does not. The morally relevant question is, is this a choice to unite biologically with one's spouse (in which case certain behaviors must be performed to carry out that choice), or is it a choice merely to give and receive sexual stimulation for some extrinsic purpose (pleasure, signifying an emotion, etc.)? If one wishes to embody a personal communion, then mere sexual stimulation (whether to orgasm or not) does not do that. By contrast, a man and a woman can unite biologically and actualize their marital communion by having sexual intercourse, that is, by performing the act that would cause procreation if the nonbehavioral conditions of procreation obtained. When performed as an expression and embodiment of their distinctively marital friendship, the act consummates their marriage on its first occasion and actualizes and enables them more fully to experience their marital communion on subsequent occasions.

appropriate for), conceiving and rearing children, that to which
the biological difference between men and women is oriented.
Hence the biological union of a husband and a wife can embody
or make present their multileveled (bodily, emotional, intellectual, volitional) marital communion. Since the biological union
is present both in sexual intercourse that results in procreation
and in sexual intercourse that does not, it follows that a married couple – a husband and a wife, whether fertile or infertile –
can choose their sexual act as embodying their marriage and thus
as instantiating an irreducible aspect of their well-being and fulfillment – a basic human good. By contrast, sexual acts that do
not establish a biological union cannot embody marriage and do
not directly realize any other basic good. A personal communion can be actualized or enhanced only by the joint sharing in
a basic good. But two or more people merely stimulating each
other to orgasm – no matter what they subjectively intend, or
how they *perceive* or *feel* their act – is not an instance of organic
unity and is not the shared realization of any basic human good.
Therefore such acts do not, in truth, realize or enhance personal
communion.

Nonmarital Sexual Acts, Multiple Partners, Incest, Bestiality...

Even today, most people recognize that incest, bestiality, and
pedophilia, as well as promiscuity and group sex, are morally
wrong. Nevertheless, it is not clear how such activities could
be immoral if the explanation of the meaning and nature of
sexual acts proposed by those opposing our view were correct.
We have shown that sexual acts, when morally right, are not just
signs or gestures of affection but actualize and embody marital
communion. But if the sexual act *were* essentially just a sign or
gesture of affection, then it is hard to see why it would *not* be an
appropriate sign to express to one's child, by an adult to his or
her friend of minor age, or even to one's pet. (After all, we hug
children and pets to comfort them or as signs of affection, and
no one supposes that there is anything wrong with that.) If sex is
essentially only a sign or gesture of affection, then why would it

be improper to use it to express one's gratitude to one's parents or one's teachers? No one sees anything wrong with sharing beautiful music with such people, or with sharing a meal with several people at one sitting. Some parents at times give their children massages, to relax them or to help them sleep if they are extremely tense. But what is it about sex that makes it improper in such circumstances?

Our point here is not a slippery slope argument. We are not predicting what acceptance of extramarital sex will lead to – though the social consequences of ideas are indeed important. Rather, our point is a strictly logical one. If incest, bestiality, polyamory, and so on, *are* morally wrong, then there must be some feature, or features, of sex that distinguishes it from activities that *are* appropriately shared with children, one's parents, in groups, and so on. But what is that feature or features? Being an intense and pleasurable sign of affection or even a mutual desire to be desired – the only traits distinctive of sex according to many who oppose our view – provides no reason to refrain from sexual acts in those contexts. Our view, on the contrary, provides an intelligible answer. What makes sexual acts distinctive and profoundly morally significant is their link to procreation and organic unity. Sexual acts are such that *either* they embody a marital communion – a communion that is sexually embodied only in reproductive-type acts between a man and a woman, in a marital relationship – *or* they involve a choice to pursue an empty or illusory experience, apart from any genuine good.

Replying to this argument (as presented in earlier works of ours), John Corvino contends that it oversimplifies what nontraditionalists on sexual morality hold about sexual acts. He writes, "First, Lee and George seem to be contrasting their view with a straw man. This is partly because the phrase 'intense and pleasurable sign of affection' oversimplifies the good(s) their opponents attribute to sex."[16] It is true that proponents of the morality

---

[16] John Corvino, "Homosexuality and the PIB Argument," *Ethics* 115 (2005): 524; by "PIB argument," Corvino means the "polygamy/incest/bestiality argument." Corvino returns to the issue in his *What's Wrong with Homosexuality?*, 121–37; however, this later treatment is less detailed than his earlier article.

of nonmarital sex wax eloquently about the goods supposedly achieved by nonmarital sex. It also is true that many people *hope to* achieve or enhance a real personal unity by nonmarital sex acts. Corvino claims that a nonmarital sexual act "can realize a shared experience of intimacy, one that is unachievable alone."[17] He says that a sexual act (whether marital or extramarital, heterosexual or homosexual) "can be a powerful and unique way of building, celebrating, and replenishing love in a relationship."[18] But these assertions only amount to claims that the sexual act enhances the personal relationship. The question is, *how* does it (allegedly) do so?

As we said earlier, an interpersonal communion can be enhanced only *in* or *by* a common pursuit or enjoyment of a substantive good, an activity or condition that is already genuinely fulfilling. What substantive good is instantiated in extramarital sex, the common pursuit or enjoyment of which is personally unifying? If the sexual act is not chosen because it actualizes and embodies a multileveled, marital communion, then one can only say that it is a sign or gesture of love (and if love, why not simply affection?) or a sharing of pleasure. But then the problem remains: if the sexual act is in its immediate reality only a sign or gesture of affection, or a sharing of pleasure, then why restrict it to mature people in a stable (or quasi-stable?) friendship? Why not allow it as an appropriate sign, or as pleasure, to share with one's children, multiple partners, or pets?

Corvino's attempted explanation of the immorality of adult-child incest – rather than answering traditionalist worries, as he intends – actually illustrates further the profound difficulties in the liberal, or nontraditionalist, view of sex. Corvino discusses the practice of males in the Etoro tribe, who require adolescent males to perform fellatio on the adults of the tribe, ostensibly because they believe the ingestion of seminal fluid is necessary

---

[17] Ibid., 520.
[18] Ibid., 512. Also see Michael Perry, "The Morality of Homosexual Conduct: A Response to John Finnis," *Notre Dame Journal of Law, Ethics, and Public Policy* 9 (1994): 51.

for maturation. Corvino says that the Etoro practice could be morally innocent given that their intentions are structured by their mistaken biological beliefs. However, Corvino claims, given the significance that sex has in our culture, adult-child incest is morally wrong. His explanation is as follows:

> Our society has certain attitudes toward both intergenerational and intrafamilial sex. Those attitudes partially result from the harms that such sex can cause, but they also partially (and indirectly) cause some of those harms. Because sex has a particular meaning in our culture, participants in incest here are subject to certain psychological and social difficulties that their analogues in Etoro society are not. That fact gives incest a moral significance here that it might well lack for the Etoro. Since the persons in question in this example are children, we should be especially careful about protecting them from these difficulties.[19]

But this explanation is manifestly weak. In the first place, if the "moral significance" of the sexual act that makes it inappropriate and harmful for adult-child incest is a result of society's attitudes, then a proponent of such relations could simply argue that those particular attitudes of society should change. Second, Corvino has failed to specify what in our society's attitudes has that effect. The problem is just pushed back to the level of societal attitudes. Other than our society's continuing disapproval of incest (which would not by itself be sufficient to condemn it),[20] and our society's persisting belief that sex should, ideally, be between a husband and a wife, what societal attitude (or attitudes) could make adult-child incest necessarily inappropriate or harmful? Corvino has failed to show why, consistently with his overall view of sexual ethics, adult-child incest should be morally excluded.

If marriage and sex are related as we have argued previously, one can easily see that marriage is the type of relationship that is incompatible with its parties also being parent and child, even

[19] Corvino, "Homosexuality and the PIB Argument," 530.
[20] A proponent of such acts could simply reply that this is an inconsistency on the part of our society. If our society adopts the attitude that sexual acts are essentially only symbols or gestures of affection, or even of love, the proponent of adult-child incest may argue that consistency demands an eventual acceptance of such acts.

when children have become adults. The marital relationship is by its nature the kind of personal communion that is consummated by bodily-sexual union and that is extended by conceiving and rearing children together. But the parent-child relationship is oriented to the development or maturation of the child. This kind of relationship is different and incompatible with the bodily, emotional, and spiritual union that is oriented toward lifelong communion and service to children of that union. Marriage is a relation of equality and mutuality, oriented both to each other and *ad extra* toward children (in the relationship's fullness). Sexual acts are of themselves oriented toward realizing – consummating or renewing – that marital relationship. Hence the sexual act tends to displace the parent-child relationship and rob the child of his or her childhood, and thus involves a grave betrayal of the trust included as part of the parent-child relationship. But since sexual liberals have not specified an intelligible good that sex must be for, and because they deny that sexual acts should be integrated with self-giving in marriage, they cannot appeal to such an argument to exclude the morality of incest.[21]

Even Corvino's argument against bestiality illustrates the inability of the liberal view of sex to provide intelligible reasons to exclude such acts. Corvino writes:

I have argued that, prima facie, homosexuality appears capable of realizing the same goods as nonprocreative heterosexual relationships.

---

[21] We may also briefly address the question of incest between siblings. This, too, we believe is excluded because of the nature of the marital good, this time the marital good as including family. The optability of sexual relations (and so of marriage) between close-in members of the family is generically hostile to the maintenance of the kind of friendship and interdependence appropriate between siblings and between parent and child. This argument is not consequentialist. What excludes incest is not the particular outcomes. Rather, the structure of the good of marriage (which is determined by its orientation to procreation and to the kind of relationship that is – or would be – intrinsically fulfilled by conceiving and raising children together) provides the required content of the form of life to be projected, intended, chosen, and lived out as a permanent and exclusive commitment of spouses. Again, such considerations are not available to those who embrace contemporary liberal doctrines about sex and marriage.

Bestiality is not comparable on this score, since (virtually by definition) it does not provide the same opportunity for interpersonal communication, intimacy, and so on.[22]

But this argument is beside the point and, thus, begs the question. Our argument is that bestiality is immoral because, obviously, there can be no personal communion between a person and a beast, and so the sexual act cannot instantiate a basic good and therefore involves a depersonalization of our sexuality. But if one does not hold that the sexual act should involve the instantiation of a first-level, basic good (in this case, the bodily-personal actuation and expression of marital unity), then the sexual act will be essentially a form of signification, gesture, or communication. If that is so, then why need it be inter-*personal* signification, gesture, or communication?

One might argue that it naturally expresses *personal* communion and so is inappropriate where there is none, thus morally excluding casual sex, *and* bestiality. The problem with this argument is that, unless an act signifies by means of first instantiating a reality, then there can be no moral objection to modifying what the act or gesture might naturally signify. Moreover, once sexual acts are put into the category of mere signs or gestures, proponents of bestiality (and of what Andrew Sullivan has approvingly described as "the spirituality of anonymous sex" – sex between strangers who do not even reveal their names or identities to each other) could deny that sexual acts naturally signify a deep personal communion, or a *personal* communion at all. They could argue that they signify *affection*, on some level or another. And on that basis, an argument could be made to defend the morality of bestiality. So, the logical point is simply that morally to exclude such acts as multiple partners, incest, and bestiality, one must defend a moral link between sex and a substantive good (such as a biological union embodying marriage, a procreative-type union) the joint participation in which actualizes a real personal communion.

[22] Corvino, "Homosexuality and the PIB Argument," 532.

In sum, choices to engage in sexual activity ought to be respectful of all of the basic human goods, in particular, the basic good of marriage. But choices to engage in sex outside marriage involve a choice contrary to the sexual integrity that is a constituent part of the good of marriage in its fullness. Such acts involve a will, or disposition in the will, that is incompatible with respect for the marital good.

5

Marriage and the Law

Two questions are central today in discussions of how the law should treat marriage. First, should the law continue to recognize marriage as essentially a relationship between a man and a woman, or should the norm of sexual complementarity be eliminated from the legal definition of marriage. Second, what stance should the law take on the issue of whether marriages are meant to be permanent?

Some Arguments for Same-sex "Marriage"

Marriage is not merely a private reality. If John and Sally get married, their marriage is publicly and legally recognized. In a great many ways, the political community will promote, protect, and encourage their relationship. But if Jim and Steve wish to get married, in most states, they will be unable to obtain a marriage license. Most states (and most nations) do not recognize same-sex "marriages." We have argued that in reality, there is no such thing as a same-sex marriage, that marriage requires a man and a woman (plus other requirements, such as proper consent). So far, however, we have discussed only the moral and social reality of marriage. One might still claim that these positions about the moral and social nature of marriage should not be enshrined in civil law. So, should the political community grant marriage

97

licenses to same-sex partners? We argue that it would be unjust and harmful for the state to do so and that the states should retain (or re-instate, as the case may be) the norm of sexual complementarity in defining marriage.

Proponents of same-sex marriage advance several arguments for their position. One argument for same-sex "marriage" is that the choice of whom to marry, including someone the same sex as oneself, is a right or liberty that government, respecting its proper limits, should not infringe. There are some areas in which the government should intervene only when absolutely necessary. Decisions about sex and whom to marry are so central to a person's identity that they fall within that area, and there is no necessity for government to enter it. So, it is argued, government should allow those who are same-sex attracted to marry the persons they love.

The second argument for this position is that a "ban" on same-sex marriage (i.e., the legal nonrecognition of same-sex partnerships as marriages) is a form of unjust discrimination. John and Sally are allowed to marry, but Jim and Steve are not: is this not treating the two couples unequally?

A third argument in favor of same-sex "marriage" – specific to the United States – is that not allowing it is unconstitutional. It is argued that not recognizing same-sex partnerships as marriages violates both the due process clause of the Fourteenth Amendment (infringing a fundamental liberty – the liberty to marry) and the equal protection clause of that same amendment.

Marriage is Prepolitical Union between a Man and a Woman

As we argued in more detail in Chapter 3, marriage is not a mere social construct, much less an individual construct. Instead, marriage is a distinct and irreducible basic human good. It is a distinctive aspect of the fulfillment or flourishing of men and women, an actualization of distinct potentialities in them. Since it is founded on human nature, and not on decisions of the state, its essential structure – the fact that it is a bodily as well as an emotional and spiritual union and that it is intrinsically oriented to procreation – cannot in reality be changed by the state. And the same is true of what is logically implied by this essential structure – namely, its exclusivity (it is between *one* man and *one* woman) and its permanence (permanence of commitment is required by the nature of marriage). Furthermore, the state has an obligation to promote, protect, and regulate marriage, because the public understanding of the nature of marriage, the actual strength (or weakness) of marriages, and the far-reaching social effects of marriages pertain in myriad ways to the public good. Just as the state has an interest in promoting and protecting health, and yet the basic structure of health cannot be changed by the state, so the state should promote marriage but cannot (and should not attempt to) change its essential nature. And just as it would be harmful and unjust for the state to obscure the nature of health by promoting false ideas about it that obscure the basic nature of health, so it is harmful and unjust for the state to promote a false view of the nature of marriage. In this chapter we explain these points.

As a prepolitical community, and as a distinct way in which human beings flourish, marriage is (1) a bodily, emotional, and spiritual union between a man and a woman – a sharing of lives on all levels of their being, including the bodily, emotional, and spiritual; and (2) the kind of union that would be naturally fulfilled by conceiving and rearing children together. It is a community that has a twofold good: the complementary and comprehensive union of the spouses and procreation and the education of children. Since marriage is oriented to the conceiving and nurturing of new *persons*, and is itself a union of persons on all levels of their being, the union of the spouses cannot be rightly viewed as merely instrumental in relation to procreation and the education of children, and so spousal union is good in itself, a genuine marriage, and an instance of a distinct basic human good – even if a given couple can achieve only the first aspect of that twofold good, given their particular circumstances.

Communities are distinguished by their purposes or common goods. So there are scholarly communities, sports communities, military communities, ordinary friendships, and so on. Marriage is distinct from other communities in that its purpose is the twofold good of the union between the spouses and the procreation and education of children (the latter being the fruition of, not the extrinsic end of, the former, as if the former were a mere means). Hence marriage is distinct from mere cohabitation. There is no intrinsic link between the union of cohabiting couples, on one hand, and the conceiving and nurturing of children, on the other. Marriage also is distinct from other cooperative unions formed only for the sake of bringing up children: neither orphanages, nor elderly sisters raising a niece or nephew, are marriages. Marriage is the type of community that is *both* a comprehensive unity (a unity on all levels of the human person, including the bodily-sexual) *and* a community naturally fulfilled by conceiving and rearing children together. Although marriage is not a mere means toward having children and bringing them up properly, it is of its nature *the kind* of relationship that would be naturally fulfilled by enlarging into a family. This is a point that is rarely adverted to in the contemporary debate about redefining marriage, but it is crucial to understanding marriage as a distinctive form of community that is not reducible to ordinary friendship or companionship.

These two essential points about marriage – that it is a bodily as well as an emotional and spiritual union and that it is oriented toward procreation – can be briefly explained as follows (also see Chapter 3). Marriage is a *bodily* union, as well as emotional and spiritual, for the sexual intercourse of a man and a woman establishes a real, biological unity: in this act, the man and the woman become biologically a single agent of a single action. Just as an individual's different organs – heart, lungs, arteries, and so forth – perform not as isolated parts but in internally coordinated unity to carry out a single biological function of the whole individual (circulation of oxygenated blood), so too in coitus the sexual organs of the male and those of the female function in a coordinated way to carry out a biological function of the couple as a unit – mating. Hence coitus establishes a real biological union with respect to this function, although it is, of course, a limited biological union inasmuch as for other functions (e.g., respiration, digestion, locomotion) the male and female remain fully distinct and self-sufficient.

The bodily, sexual aspect of the relationship is *part of* and is inherently linked to the emotional and spiritual aspects of marital communion. Human persons are not mere consciousnesses that inhabit bodies; rather, our bodies are constituent parts of us – they are part of our *personal* reality as free and rational creatures. Hence the biological unity in sexual intercourse can be (and should be) a truly *personal* unity, *the foundational part of the multileveled union that marriage distinctively is*. This biological unity embodies, makes present and able to be fully experienced, the multileveled union of the spouses in a procreative-type community. This point is indicated by the traditional doctrine – in civil law as well as ecclesiastical codes – that marriage is *consummated*, that is, the union is completed, by the spouses' sexual intercourse – by their performing the kind of act that causes children to come of their bodily union where the nonbehavioral conditions of procreation obtain.

Second, marriage is the kind of union that would be extended and naturally fulfilled by conceiving and rearing children together. The spouses' becoming mother and father, their shared parenthood, fulfills and extends their marital unity. And the child himself or herself is the concrete fruit and most profound expression of their marital commitment and their love for one another. Thus, as a form of human relationship, marriage is intrinsically oriented to procreation – but not as a mere means in relation to an extrinsic end. The spouses' bond to one another in a relationship whose distinctive structure is what it is because of its aptness for procreation and the rearing of children is no mere instrumental good but is rather good in itself – an intrinsic fulfillment of those united in the relationship.

It is often objected that marriage cannot be distinguished by its orientation toward procreation because people who are infertile – say, octogenarians – can marry. However, on the view we have just summarized, it is clear that the union of the spouses is not a mere means in relation to procreation; rather, it is the kind of union that would be fulfilled by becoming a family. Hence a marriage is and remains a genuine marriage even if procreation does not result and even if the spouses know that it will not result. With or without children, spouses are in a relationship of the type that is especially apt for procreation and would naturally be fulfilled by their having and rearing children together – their children (if they were to have children) would be embodiments of their marital communion. The marital communion of the spouses is good in itself and as such provides a noninstrumental reason for conjugal relations – relations by which they fulfill the behavioral conditions of procreation, thus giving bodily expression to their total marital union – whether or not they are capable of conceiving children (in other words, whether or not the nonbehavioral conditions of procreation happen to obtain for them); but marital communion is also naturally fulfilled when it becomes part of a larger community, the family.

Because of what marriage is, it can obtain only between a man and a woman; it is the union of sexually complementary persons who make a commitment to unite as such and live in a form of communion with each other shaped by norms (monogamy, fidelity, permanence of commitment) that follow from the kind of partnership marriage is. Same-sex partners, whatever the character or intensity of their emotional bond, cannot form together the kind of union that marriage is. To marry, a couple must, in principle, be able to form a real bodily union – not just an emotional or spiritual union, as partners in a nonsexual friendship can. And to marry, a couple must form the kind of communion that would be naturally fulfilled by conceiving and rearing children together. Same-sex couples are unable to do either of these things: the sexual acts that persons of the same sex can perform on each other do not make them biologically one (their sex acts cannot and do not under any circumstances constitute the behavioral component of procreation or fulfill its behavioral conditions) and so cannot establish the bodily foundation for the multileveled union that is marriage. And same-sex partners cannot form a union that would be naturally fulfilled by conceiving and rearing children together: they (two or more) can form sexual arrangements, and can also form alliances for child rearing, but the one relationship is distinct from, and not inherently linked to, the other.

The State Should Promote Real Marriage, Not a Counterfeit

There are two main questions about what the state should do regarding same-sex "marriage." First, provided that the state does promote and regulate marriage, should the state declare that marriage is only between a man and a woman, or might the state – whether in an effort to be fair or in an effort to be neutral – declare both same-sex and opposite-sex couples to be married? Second, could the state avoid the issue altogether? That is, does the state even need to promote and protect marriage and thus select one definition of marriage over another? Is marriage in the state's interest? Could marriage be privatized? In this section we answer these questions.

Marriage has a unique nature. Ordinary friendships can be quite temporary – say, the length of time on an airplane ride. They need not involve sharing one's whole life, and there usually is no formal agreement beginning the friendship ("I take you to be my friend.") Mere contracts – though different from ordinary friendships in many respects – are also typically temporary and need not involve all areas of the lives of those entering them. The contents of most mere contracts are malleable; that is, most items in a mere contract are *negotiable*. Unlike ordinary friendships, however, contracts do involve formal agreement, even if not written. Marriage is quite different from both of these types of agreement or union. Since marriage is a procreative-type community, it should be a sharing of whole lives, a union on all levels of the spouses' being, and, as a consequence, both exclusive and permanent.

Other characteristics in addition to exclusivity and permanence follow from the basic nature of marriage. Everyone understands that marriage and family – the latter being the fruition of the former – require devotion and take priority over most other projects. And although in exceptional cases, spouses may need to live in different cities, or spend long stretches of time apart, marriage calls for – if possible – a constant sharing of lives and a shared household.[1] Significantly, marriage has an *objective* core structure: one can enter or not enter marriage, but its basic duties follow from what it is. Moreover, marriage is more than a private agreement; by marrying, one acquires a new public status. Spouses publicly *vow* to fulfill the responsibilities that flow from the new status that marriage bestows; in marriage, the whole community – characteristically acting through a legally authorized representative – is asked to testify to the fitness of the spouses to marry (with contracts, usually only the parties to the contract testify to their ability to fulfill it). Thus, marriage is a public act, involving a public acknowledgment and celebration. Finally, it is easy for individuals to lose sight of the distinctive nature of marriage: because it is sometimes difficult to "hang in there," spouses may often be tempted to think of their marriage as if it were like an ordinary friendship (which one can let die or grow dormant, if it does not fit the rest of one's life) or as if it were a mere contract ("*She's* not living up to her part of the bargain, so why should I?").

The unique nature of marriage, considered in light of the temptations to reduce it to a (perhaps temporarily more agreeable) different type of arrangement or union, shows why the cultural understanding of marriage is so important. It also shows that, although the state should not attempt to regulate ordinary friendships at all, and should regulate contracts only indirectly, the state does have an obligation to do what it can to promote or protect a sound view of marriage. At the very least, the state has a serious obligation not to contribute to confusion about it. Because

---

[1] The minimal component of many communities, including marriage, is a set of rights and duties. If the spouses live in different cities, the community in a robust sense includes a mutual love and commitment in the will of each, memories, thought of one another, and so on. Even if the spouses live in different cities and have become existentially at odds with one another, the minimal element of the marriage persists, namely, the rights and duties to each other, to build up the marital community when it becomes possible and reasonable to do so. It is in this sense that a marriage continues even though the parties may have separated and may even have contempt for each other.

of these distinct features of marriage, the public understanding of marriage – in a way that is quite different from the public understanding of ordinary friendship or contracts – is of profound public interest and is vital to people's ability to participate in the good of marriage. The culture will either help to clarify, or contribute to confusing, the nature of this profound human and social good. The state's laws and policies partly shape the general culture. If the state conveys a gravely distorted view of marriage, it will weaken and undermine its members' capacities for full and rich participation in this critical aspect of human flourishing.

Hence the state should adopt and shape its laws and policies in line with a basically sound view of what marriage is. In particular, it must not obscure the nature of marriage by equating it with other, essentially different arrangements. Suppose the state (through its laws, policies, and educational curricula) endorsed disinformation and sophistry – counterfeits of the pursuit of knowledge. By doing so, the state would gravely harm the moral environment by which society helps or hinders the moral development and character of its members. The state would send the message that one need not respect the good of truth, that it is normal and acceptable to subordinate one's reasoning, in disregard for truth, to the attainment of other ends – which of course is just what sophistry is. In that way, the state would gravely damage the interests and violate the rights of its citizens.

Likewise, by redefining marriage in order to include same-sex partnerships, the state would confuse what the central core of marriage is. Same-sex "marriage" is possible only if marriage does not essentially include a bodily union, and it is possible only if marriage is not naturally oriented to procreation.[2] So,

---

[2] Writing the majority opinion in *Goodridge* (which overturned Massachusetts's traditional marriage law), Justice Marshal described marriage as follows: "While it is certainly true that many, perhaps most, married couples have children (assisted or unassisted), *it is the exclusive and permanent commitment of the marriage partners to one another, not the begetting of children, that is the sine qua non of civil marriage.*" Goodridge v. Dept. of Public Health, 798 N.E.2d 941 (Mass. 2003) Similarly, when striking down Proposition 8

redefining marriage in order to include same-sex partnerships would convey the message that, instead of being a conjugal union with a core objective structure, a union both good in itself and intrinsically oriented to procreation, marriage is a relationship principally defined by emotional connection, the exchange of sexual pleasure, and shared housekeeping (important but nonetheless ancillary features or consequences of marriage and not specific to it). This would undermine the public understanding of marriage and erode respect for the genuine human good of marriage. In a misguided effort to "expand" access to marriage, the state would be abolishing marriage and replacing it with some other sort of arrangement – sexual-romantic companionship or domestic partnership to which the label "marriage" is then reassigned.

In sum, marriage is the kind of human good that can be chosen and realized only by persons who have some basic understanding of what it essentially is. Hence creating a culture that obscures the nature of marriage and, thus, its central and defining features, makes it more difficult to participate in, cultivate, and appreciate genuine marriage.

The argument we are presenting differs importantly from the way the marriage-as-procreative argument is often proposed. It is sometimes argued that the state's interest in marriage is simply to ensure that as many children as possible are raised in "an optimal setting" and that this interest justifies "restricting" marriage to opposite-sex couples. But the fact that intact homes are the optimal setting for child rearing does not *by itself* justify a policy of recognizing only opposite-sex partnerships as marriages. For

(which reestablished conjugal marriage under California law after it had been invalidated by that state's supreme court), in *Perry v. Schwarzenegger*, Judge Vaughn Walker described marriage as follows: "Marriage requires two parties to give their free consent to form a relationship, which then forms the foundation of a household" (111). He added, "The spouses must consent to support each other and any dependents." Perry v. Schwarzenegger, 704 F. Supp. 2d 921, 1003 (N.D. Cal. 2010). Note, however, that this obligation of support makes sense only if marriage is as we have described it earlier. It is groundless – a mere arbitrary addition to make the new definition appear less disruptive than it is – if marriage is as Judge Walker describes it.

a good end (ensuring optimal care for children) would not justify the means (excluding same-sex "marriage") if it could be shown that the means were unjust – and denying marriage to such couples, if they were able to form a true marital partnership, *would be* unjust. The core of our argument, however, is that marriage is by its nature conjugal union – a distinctively comprehensive (bodily as well as emotional) sharing of life made possible by the sexual-reproductive complementarity of man and woman and naturally oriented toward procreation and the rearing of children. Its unique and profound aptness for the nurturing and educating of children – the thing that grounds the *public* interest in marriage as an institution and its *legal* recognition and regulation – follows from its nature as a conjugal partnership. Precisely as a conjugal bond, marriage brings together a man and woman as husband and wife to be mother and father to any children who may come of their union, providing those children, if all goes well, with the inestimable blessing of being brought up in the monogamous and faithful bond of the mother and father to whom (and to whose larger families) they are related in the most comprehensive way: biologically as well as emotionally.

Moreover, advancing the "optimal setting" argument as if it by itself establishes what marriage is locates the center of debate in the wrong place. Doing so might make it seem as if the whole issue (of whether the state should redefine marriage) hinged on the outcome of sociological studies comparing children raised in opposite-sex parental households to children raised in same-sex parental households. Now at this point it has become quite clear – after decades of social research studies – that in general, children fare better when they are raised by their married biological parents, as compared to single mothers, cohabitors, or ex-spouses sharing custody.[3] The studies that

---

[3] Susan L. Brown, "Family Structure and Child Well-Being: The Significance of Parental Cohabitation," *Journal of Marriage and Family* 66 (2004): 351–67; Wendy Manning, Pamela Smock, and Debarun Majumdar, "The Relative Stability of Cohabiting and Marital Unions for Children," *Population Research and Policy Review* 23 (2004): 135–59; Sara McLanahan and Gary Sandefur, *Growing Up with a Single Parent: What Hurts, What Helps* (Cambridge, MA: Harvard University Press, 1994).

directly compare children raised by same-sex partners to children raised by opposite-sex, married couples are fewer and more recent. Many such studies have methodological problems (e.g., very small samples, nonrepresentative samples, merely subjective measurements of well-being) and may have been shaped by bias.[4] One of the largest and methodologically most reliable studies does suggest that children raised by a parent who is in or has been in a same-sex romantic relationship in general fared significantly *poorer* than children who grew up in biologically intact mother-father families, with respect to several measures of well-being, including academic success, employment success, mental well-being (depression), and relationship security.[5]

Nevertheless, the question of how well or badly same-sex partners do by reference to standard indicators (educational attainment, juvenile delinquency, substance abuse, suicidal ideation, etc.) in rearing children is not determinative of whether the state should recognize same-sex partnerships as marriages. (It is more relevant to questions regarding adoption by same-sex partners than to the question of what marriage is and how it should be legally defined.) For even if same-sex parents raised children as well or better than opposite-sex married couples, still, redefining marriage would not only obscure its nature but damage serious interests of children. For the view of marriage it would convey ("marriage" as sexual-romantic companionship or domestic

---

4 Steven Nock, Affidavit of Steven Nock re Halpern et al. v. Canada and MCCT v. Canada, Ontario S.C.D.C., http://marriagelaw.cua.edu/Law/cases/Canada/ontario/halpern/aff_nock.pdf; Mark Regnerus, "How Different Are the Adult Children of Parents Who Have Same-Sex Relationships? Findings from the New Family Structures Study," *Social Science Research* 41 (2012): 752–53, http://www.sciencedirect.com/science/article/pii/S0049089X12000610; Loren Marks, "Same-Sex Parenting and Children's Outcomes: A Closer Examination of the American Psychological Association's Brief on Lesbian and Gay Parenting," *Social Science Research* 41 (2012): 735–51, http://www.sciencedirect.com/science/article/pii/S0049089X12000580. For a review of the research in the last few decades, see *Ten Principles on Marriage and the Public Good*, signed by some seventy scholars, at http://protectmarriage.com/wp-content/uploads/2012/11/WI_Marriage.pdf.
5 Regnerus, "How Different Are the Adult Children of Parents Who Have Same-Sex Relationships?," esp. 763–66.

partnership) would, sooner or later, result in even more children being conceived outside wedlock, more children raised in broken homes, and all that follows for children and society when these things become common. Although the social function of marriage does not by itself constitute or establish what it is, real marriage *does* perform the absolutely crucial social function of encouraging fathers to commit to their children and the mothers of their children and to fulfill their moral responsibilities to them. Children come to be in a dependent and vulnerable condition and so need to be loved, nurtured, and protected. They can usually count on their mothers to care for them when they are young; for, although both the mother and the father are morally responsible to the child they have jointly brought into being, fathers are more likely than mothers to shirk that responsibility (especially if there is little or no cultural pressure to fulfill it). This is partly because it is the mother, not the father, who nurtures the child within her body for nine months, almost always develops a close, natural bond of affection with the child, and will inevitably be present when the child is born. But a strong marriage culture links fathers also to their children (and their children's mothers). The institution of marriage provides the normative link between coitus and procreation, on one hand, and responsibilities to the family – especially on the part of the husband-father – on the other hand. Where the nature of marriage is obscured and the culture of marriage is weakened, fewer young men and women marry, fewer view marriage as the proper context for sexual conduct and expression, and the number of children born outside marriage dramatically increases, and with it the number of children growing up outside intact families. But both common sense and social science research indicate that generally, children fare best, on virtually every indicator of well-being, when raised by their married biological parents.[6]

Severing the idea of marriage from any intrinsic link to procreation, and identifying it as an essentially emotional union, diminishes the appreciation of the distinctive value of marriage

---

[6] See note 3.

and of the rationale for the norms of exclusivity and permanence. That in turn gravely harms spouses, but especially children. Thus, while marriage is not a mere means created by the state to provide a suitable environment for the begetting and raising of children, the institution of marriage does provide this crucial social function. For this reason the state has a heightened interest – a heightened obligation – to promote a healthy marriage culture. A false notion of marriage has harmful social effects. These points remain true independently of whether the comparatively few same-sex couples do or do not raise children well.

Someone might argue that the state should remain neutral and that it can do so by declaring both same-sex and opposite-sex couples civilly married, and so not adopting one moral view over against others. However, redefining marriage to include same-sex partnerships would not be a neutral act. This would publicly equate certain same-sex relationships with genuine marriages (i.e., marriages that are truly conjugal unions) and so it would be a public adoption and endorsement of a certain view of marriage, namely, that marriage does not essentially include a real bodily union and is not naturally oriented to procreation. The state would send the message that the essential core of marriage is an emotional union (with a commitment to some degree of stability and ordinarily a shared household), and it would make nonsense of the idea that marriage should be permanent (as a matter of principle and not mere sentiment or subjective preference) or necessarily involve, as a matter of principle, sexual exclusivity and fidelity. Thus, the state cannot remain neutral regarding the public understanding of what marriage is. Its laws regarding marriage will inevitably promote one view or another (the conjugal view or some alternative view) of what marriage is.

These points also show that the state cannot ignore marriage. Some have argued that the state could remain neutral on the same-sex "marriage" issue by withdrawing from the certification and licensing of marriages altogether. In this way the state could leave it to different religions or different groups with different worldviews to devise their ceremonies, and so marriage would be a nonpolitical reality, somewhat as baptisms or bar mitzvahs are now.

But there are decisive reasons against this proposal. First, it does not even seem possible for the state to avoid having to regulate marriage. For, though marriage is more than a contract, it still is one (it is more, not less, than a contract), and one that generates responsibilities and liabilities specific to marriage rather than to any other kind of contract. Hence the state must set some standards and adjudicate some disputes about marriage, in particular those pertaining to property, inheritance, and child custody. So, the state cannot avoid distinguishing between who is and who is not married.

To this, one might reply that marriage could be a private contract publicly enforced but have different responsibilities and liabilities in different cases. But this would leave open the question being debated – namely, whether opposite-sex marriage contracts should be equated to same-sex "marriage-like" contracts – and the controversy will not have been avoided.

Second – as is clear from what we have said earlier – even if it were possible for the state to retreat from marriage licensing, this would constitute a serious failure regarding central responsibilities belonging to any political community. The state exists in order to promote ends that (1) serve interests that are widely shared within that society and (2) can effectively and appropriately be pursued by political society (unlike ends that can best be pursued only by individuals, families, or voluntary associations). The *public good* is constituted by such ends. The public good clearly includes defending against external attacks, preserving internal order, establishing just terms of social interaction, facilitating transportation, and providing a judicial system for fair resolution of disputes. Omitting to do any of these would be grave injustices. But the public good also includes the promotion, protection, and regulation of marriage – as has been recognized in virtually every complex political society.

This is true for at least three reasons. First, a clear public or cultural understanding of marriage – as we have shown – helps to convey to young men and women, as well as those already married, the distinctive and irreducible value of marriage and renders its norms intelligible, just as a clear public understanding of health or learning assists families and individuals in those areas. Second, a healthy institution of marriage – where marriage is esteemed and people who enter it understand the point of its norms and appreciate its serious responsibilities – is beneficial especially to children and their mothers. Third, married couples raise the next generation, schooling them in virtue and social responsibility; most of this care and work is not monetarily compensated. Hence a failure to attach benefits and privileges to married couples is an injustice – a failure to encourage and reward a unique and vital social function.

Replies to Some Arguments for Same-sex "Marriage"

In the introduction to this chapter we mentioned three arguments commonly advanced to support redefining marriage to include some same-sex partnerships. We return now to reply explicitly to those objections. The first argument we mentioned is that decisions about sex and whom to marry are so central to a person's identity that government should enter that area of privacy only if necessary, and banning same-sex "marriage" intrudes into this area without necessity. Our reply is that this objection, though common, is based on a fundamental confusion about the question regarding the state's redefinition of marriage. If two people cohabit and regularly have sex, then they might claim that their actions are merely private. But what proponents of same-sex "marriage" demand is not something private – the liberty regarding private acts was granted when states repealed antisodomy laws and when remaining laws prohibiting sodomy were struck down by the Supreme Court case *Lawrence v. Texas* in 2003.

The issue here is not what those with same-sex attractions are or are not allowed to do but what the political community will do (what it will recognize and promote as marriages). What same-sex "marriage" proponents demand is public endorsement of same-sex sexual relationships by the political community, a public affirmation by the political community that a sexual relationship with some degree of commitment, and perhaps a shared household, is equivalent to marriage as historically, and, we believe, rightly, understood. A decision by the political community not to make such an endorsement, and not to make such a false declaration, does nothing whatsoever to limit the liberty of those who wish to form such relationships.

Thus, it is misleading and prejudicial to speak of a "ban on same-sex marriage" and to describe the issue as if the question were whether the state should continue to prohibit same-sex marriages. In fact, no states prohibit same-sex couples from entering a relationship they deem (mistakenly) to be marriage or to get a minister or other authority to pronounce it as such. The state laws on marriage do not prohibit same-sex couples from doing anything – their liberty is not restricted by the state at all, much less any fundamental liberty restricted. What is at issue is whether *we* as a political community will be compelled to affirm that their relationship is fully equivalent to marriage.[7]

---

[7] Justice Anthony Kennedy's descriptions of marriage in the opinion he wrote for the majority's holding in the Supreme Court's U.S. v. Windsor, 570 U.S. (2013), at 20, inadvertently show that the issue is not the liberty of same-sex partners but the endorsement by the political community of their choices: "For same-sex couples who wished to be married, the State [of New York] acted to give their lawful conduct a lawful status. This status is a far-reaching acknowledgment of the intimate relationship between two people, a relationship deemed by the State worthy of dignity in the community equal with all other marriages." Thus, the question is not whether the state or the federal government (and it was only the federal government's actions at issue, not the state governments' action) will limit the liberty of same-sex people seeking marriage but whether the political community – the State – will take it as a public and official position that the difference between opposite-sex couples and same-sex couples is irrelevant to what marriage is.

Justice Kennedy's descriptions of the status of marriage for same-sex couples also show – despite his intentions – how the movement to redefine marriage laws is an attempt by a small group to subvert those laws for its own private ends, ends that are quite distinct from what the state's purpose in promoting marriage has ever been. The state's interest in marriage has never been to affirm intimate romantic connections as such. Rather, the state's interest has always been the joining of mothers and fathers to each other and to whatever children they might have.

The second and perhaps best known argument mentioned previously is that, for the state to grant marriage licenses to opposite-sex couples, but refuse to grant them to same-sex couples, is to treat a class of people – those with same-sex attractions – unequally. Or as a Republican state senator from New York recently argued – explaining why he voted in favor of same-sex "marriage" – "I cannot deny a person, a human being . . . the same rights that I have with my wife." And of course, the slogan for the same-sex "marriage" movement is "marriage equality."

However, to treat classes of people differently is not always *unjust* discrimination. For the law to treat different classes differently is not unjust if the difference between those classes is relevant to a legitimate purpose of the state. For example, as Justice Alito pointed out in his dissenting opinion in *U.S. v. Windsor*, a law that forbids women from being the executors of an estate is unjust because being male or female is irrelevant to executing an estate. But statutory rape laws that criminalize sexual intercourse with a woman under the age of eighteen years but do not similarly criminalize partners of underage men is not unjust, since the difference between men and women is intelligibly related to the purpose of the law. For, "young men and young women are not similarly situated with respect to the problems and the risks of sexual intercourse."[8] Or again, treating those already married differently than those who are not yet married and otherwise eligible for marriage (denying the first group marriage licenses but not the second group) does not *unjustly* discriminate against those who are already married, since the difference between already being married and not yet being married is crucially relevant to the purpose of issuing marriage licenses.

The argument based on equality or justice that marriage must be redefined, then, presupposes that opposite-sex couples and same-sex partners are similarly situated with respect to the possibility of marriage – and that therefore "allowing" the first to

---

[8] This example is taken from Justice Alito's dissenting opinion in U.S. v. Windsor, 570 U.S. (2013), at 12. The quote is from Michael M. v. Superior Court, Sonoma City, 450 U.S. 463, 471 (1981) (plurality opinion).

marry but not the second must be based on animus or bigotry. But the distinction between opposite-sex couples and same-sex couples – as we have shown – is indeed relevant to the nature and purposes of marriage. Same-sex partners are unable to form the kind of union marriage is. And so the state's not granting same-sex partners marriage licenses is simply a decision by the state not to engage in a confusing and harmful fiction. Marriage is a certain kind of bond – a conjugal union. Hence declining to offer or grant a marriage license, or the privileges, protections, and obligations of marriage, to nonmarital partnerships, be they same-sex, bigamous, polyamorous, or what have you, is not unjust discrimination. The state denies marriage licenses to polyamorous people who form sexual threesomes or foursomes (refraining from recognizing their sexual partnerships as marriages), and it denies marriage licenses to twelve-year-olds (requiring valid consent for a marriage). These denials are not unjust because threesomes, foursomes, and twelve-year-olds cannot form the kind of union that marriage is. But the same is true of same-sex twosomes.

The third argument we mentioned at the beginning of this chapter was that denying marriage licenses to same-sex couples violates the Constitution of the United States. The argument has been that recognizing only opposite-sex marriage violates both the due process clause and the equal protection clause of the Fourteenth Amendment. We examine both parts of this argument in turn.

The Fourteenth Amendment says in part, "Nor shall any State deprive any person of life, liberty, or property, without due process of law." Of course, almost every law deprives some persons of liberty. To understand what restrictions upon government (state and federal) this amendment imposes, one must determine what "due process of law" means. This phrase has been interpreted as having substantive, not just procedural, meaning. That is, the amendment does more than say *how* government (state or federal) may limit liberty (say, by written and promulgated statutes); it also says that there are certain liberties themselves (in addition to those specifically enumerated in the other

constitutional provisions, such as freedom of speech and freedom
of religion) that government may not restrict (except, perhaps,
for the gravest reasons). Such liberties are called *fundamental*,
and they include the right or liberty to have children, to direct
the upbringing of one's children, to bodily integrity, and to refuse
medical treatment.[9]

For example, in *Griswold v. Connecticut* (1965), the U.S.
Supreme Court held that married individuals have a right to make
certain decisions about marital intimacy, including a decision to
use contraceptives (a later decision, *Eisenstadt v. Baird* [1971],
held that unmarried individual also possess this right). However,
not all rights or liberties can be classified as protected by the due
process clause in the Fourteenth Amendment. As noted in several
Supreme Court cases, only *fundamental* rights or liberties are to
have this heightened protection (i.e., requiring what the courts
call a "compelling state interest" to be restricted). Otherwise,
the judiciary would be completely unrestrained, as it could count
any liberty as fundamental and impose its own views of what
social policy should be. So it is only fundamental rights or liberties – including those directly specified, or implied, by the Bill
of Rights – that deserve heightened protection. A fundamental
right or liberty is defined as one that is "deeply rooted in this
Nation's history and tradition" or that is "implicit in the concept of ordered liberty."[10] Thus, the Supreme Court held that the
right to refuse medical treatment was a fundamental liberty or
right but rejected the claim that there was a fundamental right to
physician-assisted suicide. Same-sex marriage proponents argue
that the right to marry is a fundamental right or liberty and that
this right includes the right to marry the person of one's choice,
including someone of the same sex.

Under prevailing constitutional jurisprudence, the choice to
marry is a fundamental right, and the choice to marry the person

[9] See William Rehnquist's majority opinion in Washington v. Glucksberg, 521
U.S. (1997), at 702.
[10] Palko v. Connecticut, 302 U.S. 319 (1937). In *Glucksberg*, Rehnquist added
that the protected liberty must also have a "careful description," by which
he meant specific or not too general, but we are not concerned with that
requirement here. See Washington v. Glucksberg, 521 U.S. (1997), Part II.

of one's choice (with that person's consent) is part of this right. But of course, the concrete meaning of this right depends on what marriage is and how it is defined by law. If one is already married, one does not have a fundamental right to marry a second wife or husband (laws against polygamy have been upheld as constitutional). That's because the Constitution does not forbid the states to recognize that marriage is a conjugal union and to legally define it, therefore, as the union of one man and one woman in an exclusive bond. Of course, the state may not forbid someone from marrying someone else (or refuse to recognize a marriage) where the prospective spouses can form a conjugal union. That is why laws forbidding interracial marriages are not only unjust but unconstitutional. There is no reason why spouses of different races cannot form a comprehensive (bodily as well as emotional) union that is naturally ordered to procreation and would naturally be fulfilled by their having and rearing children together. In truth, antimiscegenation laws were pure products of a system of white supremacy and racial subordination and were designed precisely to reinforce that system – one in which blacks were held in a position of socioeconomic inferiority and rendered vulnerable to exploitation. Nothing remotely like this is true of the laws historically establishing marriage as the conjugal union of husband and wife.

Moreover, the argument that restricting marriage to opposite-sex couples infringes a fundamental liberty begs the question. It presupposes that there *is* such a thing as marrying someone of the same sex, and *that is precisely what is at issue.* If marriage is a certain type of relation – in reality, and not just by legal fiat – and if by its nature it is a man-woman relationship, then the *liberty* of same-sex couples, whether fundamental or not, has not been infringed at all by the state's defining marriage as a conjugal union. This is an elementary point but crucial for the logic of the issue. The license to X depends on what X is – a license to teach does not give one permission to yell at one's neighbors at two in the morning; a license to hunt wild animals does not grant one permission to shoot a neighbor's pet dog. So, if Jones and Smith are denied a license to do X, their right was violated only if what they proposed to do really was X. The right or liberty to marry is fundamental, but it is a right *to marry*, not a right to the state's declaration that one's sexual relationship – which may be of various contours – is marriage.

The equal protection clause of the Fourteenth Amendment says that the state shall not "deny to any person within its jurisdiction the equal protection of the laws." Same-sex marriage proponents argue that refusing marriage licenses to same-sex partners, while granting them to opposite-sex couples, treats same-sex attracted persons unequally and thus denies them the constitutionally guaranteed equal protection clause.

But this argument is utterly flawed. The equal protection clause of the Constitution does not, of course, prohibit every classification or distinction. Laws characteristically classify and distinguish. The question is whether a particular classification is invidious. A classification is invidious when it is not essentially related to the purpose of the law and the law's purpose is part of the public good. (Earlier, we discussed equality with respect to justice or fairness in general; here we examine the question of what the Constitution implies.) The purpose of marriage statutes is to promote marriage – because real marriage is in itself a distinctive basic good and because a healthy marriage culture provides a social structure beneficial to the conceiving and rearing of children. But because sexual complementarity is essential to marriage properly understood, then whether a couple is opposite-sex or same-sex *is* intrinsically related to the purpose of the statute, a purpose that is part of the public good. Just as the distinction between eighteen-year-olds and twelve-year-olds is relevant to the purpose of marriage – because the former but not the latter are actually able to form the union that is marriage – in the same way, the distinction between opposite-sex couples and same-sex partners is relevant to the purpose of the marriage statute, because the former but not the latter can actually form the kind of union that marriage is.[11]

---

[11] In *U.S. v. Windsor*, the Supreme Court struck down a section of the *federal* law (the Defense of Marriage Act [DOMA], passed in 1996) that defined, for purposes of federal benefits, that marriage is only between a man and a

It will be objected to this argument that the institution of marriage has changed in the past and can change again. If same-sex partners are allowed to marry (the objection continues), the core of marriage will remain, though its definition will be broadened. For example, in the trial court decision ruling that California's pro-marriage amendment to the California Constitution violated the U.S. Constitution, Judge Vaughn Walker said, "The marital bargain in California (along with other states) traditionally required that a woman's legal and economic identity be subsumed by her husband's upon marriage under the doctrine of coverture; this once-unquestioned aspect of marriage now is regarded as antithetical to the notion of marriage as a union of equals."[12] So, the argument is that certain aspects of marriage changed, but the core of marriage remained; in the same way (it is argued), the allegedly unjust discrimination involved in

woman, and by "spouse" is meant either a husband or a wife in such relationships. This case did not strike down *state* laws (or constitutions) that define marriage as between a man and a woman. So as of this writing, states are still free to recognize that marriage is only between a man and a woman. Writing the majority opinion, Justice Kennedy assumed – without any argument whatsoever – that there was no intelligible link between the classification drawn by the law and the purpose of the law. Kennedy claimed that the federal government's defining marriage in this way inflicted on same-sex couples an "injury and indignity": "What the State of New York treats as alike [i.e., same-sex couples wishing to marry and opposite-sex couples wishing to marry] the federal law deems unlike by a law designed to injure the same class the State seeks to protect." U.S. v. Windsor 570 U.S. (2013) (majority opinion).

Amazingly, Kennedy does not examine explanations advanced by proponents of the federal law to determine whether being opposite-sex or same-sex is a relevant distinction for marriage – he does not even bother, for example, to discuss how marriage might be conceived as related to procreation. However, as Justice Alito points out in his dissenting opinion, adversaries of DOMA who invoke the equal protection clause "ask us to rule that the presence of two members of the opposite sex is as rationally related to marriage as white skin is to voting or a Y-chromosome is to the ability to administer an estate" (see U.S. v Windsor, 570 U.S. [2013] [Alito's dissenting opinion]). And on this Justice Alito comments, "That is a striking request and one that unelected judges should pause before granting. Acceptance of the argument would cast all those who cling to traditional beliefs about the nature of marriage in the role of bigots or superstitious fools."

12 Perry v. Schwarzenegger 112.

restricting marriage to opposite-sex couples can be ended, while the core of marriage remains.

There is, however, an obvious and fatal flaw in this argument by analogy. Coverture was a doctrine that directed how the family or the spouses as a couple should relate to outside agencies, especially the state. But, manifestly, rules governing how a community should relate to outside agencies – who speaks for them, whether the members are to be related to individually or as a group – presupposes the nature of the community in question (unless the precise purpose of the community is to relate to these outside agencies, something no one argues is true for marriage). By contrast, if the purpose of marriage is the twofold good of the comprehensive union of the spouses and (relatedly) the conceiving and rearing of children, then whether the individuals seeking to form that union are in principle capable of doing so is *not* incidental to the purpose of marriage statutes. That is, a change in how a community relates to outside agencies (provided how it does is not its central purpose) is quite different from a change in the fundamental purpose of a community – in fact, the proposed change is not actually a change in marriage at all but a substitution of an entirely different type of relationship or arrangement for marriage.

A similar point applies to the objection that "excluding" same-sex partners from marriage is analogous to excluding interracial couples from marriage. It is often argued that just as there were laws forbidding interracial marriages, and they were rightly struck down because they violate the equal protection clause of the Fourteenth Amendment, in the same way, excluding same-sex partners from marriage is animated by bigotry and an animus against homosexuals. However, the purpose of the race classification was transparently part of the larger system of white supremacy and exploitation designed for no other purpose than to keep African Americans in a position of political, social, and economic inferiority: the classification (distinction) is unrelated to the purpose of the marriage laws. But this is false with respect to the distinction between same-sex partners and opposite-sex couples. Being of the same sex is indeed relevant to the purpose of marriage laws – the purpose of which is to promote marriage considered precisely as a conjugal union.[13] Two people of the same sex cannot truly be married, any more than a pair of twelve-year-olds can be married – they are unable to form the kind of union marriage is: a conjugal union.

One could object that that's not what marriage is (a man-woman union of the kind that would be fulfilled by having and rearing children together). But that would require a successful argument – and so far no argument at all has been given. Questioning the motives of marriage supporters, or calling them names ("bigot," "homophobe"), or drawing flawed analogies with racist practices will not serve as substitutes for the required argument. We believe that resorting to these tactics is felt to be necessary only because no plausible argument for reconceiving marriage as a mere form of sexual-romantic companionship or domestic partnership is available.

Finally, we should mention also an argument frequently made for same-sex marriage, what one could call the "no-harm" claim. Often this is articulated in the form of rhetorical questions: "If Steve marries Jim, how will that affect John and Sally's marriage? Will John suddenly be tempted to leave Sally to take up with another man?" In showing why the state has an obligation to promote marriage and not obscure it, we have already provided the substance of an answer to this claim. However, it is worth addressing directly because we think confusion on this point partly explains why many same-sex marriage proponents so often believe that conjugal-marriage defenders are motivated by animus or bigotry. The same-sex "marriage" proponents assume that the change in marriage is only a slight one, and so when others respond by insisting that marriage not be changed in this way, they suspect there must be some other motive lurking beneath this reaction. However, we have shown that the change would indeed be fundamental – a shift from marriage conceived as essentially a bodily-emotional-spiritual bond, one naturally fulfilled by

---

[13] And as a simple matter of constitutional law, even if this question is only debatable, it should be a legislative issue, not a judicial one.

procreation and education of children (and so requiring exclusivity and the sincere pledge of permanence), to "marriage" conceived as essentially an emotional union, one not including an organic bodily union and not intrinsically linked to procreation and education of children (and one that therefore provides no principled moral basis for the requirements of exclusivity and permanence). This change would harm marriage in the same way that recognizing and promoting polyamorous partnerships would harm marriage: by changing in a fundamental way its cultural understanding. And so it would harm young men and women by making this good less available to them – since marriage needs to be understood at least in a basic way to be consented to – and would also harm children by weakening the most central institution that provides for their nurturance and education.

The Incoherence of the Same-sex "Marriage" Proposal

It is clear that what same-sex marriage supporters principally want is the social affirmation and endorsement of homosexual relationships. The evidence for that is that the concrete benefits that accrue to marriage – hospital visitation, inheritance rights, and so on – could easily be secured by other means for individuals who desire them (e.g., a durable power of attorney for health care or a will). Clearly it is not just tolerance that is desired, since persons with same-sex attractions are free to engage in private sexual behavior and are free to establish for themselves long-term romantic and sexual relationships. Rather, what is desired is public endorsement. Judge Walker expressed quite clearly this point in his decision striking down the California pro-marriage amendment: "Plaintiffs [some same-sex couples] seek to have the state recognize their committed relationships . . . Perry and Stier seek to be spouses; they seek the mutual obligation and honor that attend marriage."[14] And Judge Walker favorably quoted the following from a lower court in California: "One of the core

[14] Perry v. Schwarzenegger, 113–14.

elements of the fundamental right to marry is the right of same-sex couples to have their official family relationship accorded the same dignity, respect, and stature as that accorded to all other officially recognized family relationships."[15]

So, the proposal is for the state to promote something called marriage and that marriage be understood in a way that will include same-sex partners – all of this sounds like we are merely reporting old news. The problem is this: what is the thing called "marriage," on their view, and why should the state promote it? What distinguishes marital unions from others, such that the state should promote marriages? One cannot just pronounce that these pairs of individuals will henceforth count as *married*; there must be something one means by "being married," something held in common by all married couples. A serious problem with the same-sex "marriage" proposal is that no coherent account can be given of what that something is, and so the position is actually incoherent.

If marriage is not, as traditionally defined, a bodily, emotional, and spiritual union of a man and a woman, naturally oriented to procreation, then what makes a union marriage, and why should the state support it? Obviously, it is not simply a union that is formed by a wedding *ceremony*: that would be a circular definition; we would still need to know what makes it a *wedding* ceremony as opposed to another type. It also is obvious that marriage involves a romantic and sexual relationship, but not every romantic and sexual relationship is a marriage, and certainly there is no point in the state promoting all such relationships. Perhaps one will say that it is a *stable, committed*, and *exclusive* romantic-sexual relationship? However, the question then arises, how stable does a romantic-sexual relationship need to be in order to be a marriage? Suppose John and Sally are in a romantic-sexual relationship while college students but plan to go their separate ways after graduation: is that stable enough to be a marriage? If not, why not? Or suppose they have a stable relationship in their senior year, knowing it will last only to the

---

[15] Ibid., 114.

end of the school year seven months away (and they plan to suspend their relationship for Christmas and spring breaks): will that be stable enough? If not, why not?

Or suppose Joe, Jim, and Steve have a committed, stable, romantic-sexual relationship among themselves – a polyamorous relationship. On what ground can the state promote the relationship between couples, but not the relationship among "triads," like Joe, Jim, and Steve? The point of these questions is this: there must be some nonarbitrary features shared by relationships the state promotes that make them apt for public promotion and make it fair for the state not to promote similar relationships lacking those features. The conjugal understanding of marriage has a ready answer for that: (1) marriage is a distinct basic human good that needs social support and that uniquely provides important social functions; and (2) marriage's organic bodily union and inherent orientation to procreation distinguish it from other relationships superficially similar to it and ground in a principled way its structuring norms. But the same-sex marriage proposal's conception of marriage can provide no answer. In fact, its conception of marriage is actually an arbitrarily selected class, and so the enactment of this proposal would be unjust.

This problem is evident in the descriptions of marriage by judges when they strike down pro-marriage laws or even state constitutional amendments. In his decision striking down California's pro-marriage amendment to that state's constitution, Judge Walker described marriage as follows:

Marriage has retained certain characteristics throughout the history of the United States. Marriage requires two parties to give their free consent to form a relationship, which then forms the foundation of a household. The spouses must consent to support each other and any dependents. The state regulates marriage because marriage creates stable households, which in turn form the basis of a stable, governable populace.[16]

Of course, he also holds that the relationship must be a romantic-sexual one, for later in his decision, referring to marriage, he

---

[16] Ibid., 111.

says, "Sex and sexual orientation are necessarily interrelated, *as an individual's choice of romantic or intimate partner based on sex is a large part of what defines an individual's sexual orientation.*"[17]

So on Judge Walker's view, the state is to promote a romantic-sexual relationship between two parties who form a household and who agree to support each other and any dependents. And, he claims, the reason the state supports such relationships is that they create stable households. However, this idea of marriage is impossible to apply fairly. Recall the college students who consent to cohabit for their times on campus during their college days, sharing an apartment, not having any dependents: they would seem to qualify for marital status given Judge Walker's definition or description. And yet most people – including those students, no doubt – would say without hesitation that they are *not* married. By contrast, Jim, Joe, and Steve, in a polyamorous relationship, would *not* qualify (since Judge Walker stipulated the parties to marriage must be *two*). But apart from mere arbitrary stipulation, on what basis should the polyamorous partners be denied marital status? Surely they could argue that their relationship too *creates a stable household* – and if so, denying them marital status while granting it to couples would be unjust discrimination.

Moreover, if the basis of the state's interest in marriage is only to create stable households, then why must two (or more) people be in a romantic-sexual relationship to qualify for this status? Two elderly sisters or three celibate monks can form a stable household. If the purpose of marriage laws is simply to form stable households, then it would be inherently unjust to provide the benefits and status of marriage to those who have romantic-sexual relationships but deny them to cohabiting elderly sisters or cohabiting celibate monks.

The problem is not solved if one adds to one's description or definition of marriage that it must be a permanent commitment. In the *Goodridge* case, Chief Justice Margaret Marshall said of

---

[17] Ibid., 120; emphasis added.

marriage, "It is the exclusive and permanent commitment of the marriage partners to one another, not the begetting of children, that is the sine qua non of civil marriage."[18] But it must be asked, why *should* the commitment be exclusive and permanent? The college students' relationship (lacking permanence) and the celibate monks' relationship (lacking exclusivity – they're open to others joining their religious order) each share a household and contribute, in some measure, to social stability. By contrast, the conjugal understanding of marriage provides an easy answer to these questions: since marriage is bodily, procreative, and an irreducibly distinct basic good, it is naturally distinct from other relationships. The promotion of this kind of relationship, for its own sake (because it is a distinct basic good), and for the sake of children generally, means that it is in accord with justice to recognize relationships between two and only two spouses and to recognize only permanent and exclusive unions as marriages. In other words, the conjugal conception of marriage is coherent; the same-sex marriage proponents' conception is incoherent.

It is important to see that our argument here is not a slippery slope argument. Rather, our point is that the revisionist view of marriage doesn't make sense, that the thing it calls "marriage" is an arbitrary set. That incoherence will lead to at least two serious problems. First, to arbitrarily select for some people, but deny to others, a certain status and certain benefits is inherently unjust. There is no objective ground for conferring the status of marriage on the gerrymandered group devised by same-sex marriage supporters as qualifying for marriage (two people romantically and sexually involved, making a commitment of stability – and perhaps of permanence and exclusivity – to one another) and not polyamorous groups and households formed by couples (or trios or more) who are not romantically-sexually involved. By contrast, if in the interest of justice one drops, say, the requirement for a romantic-sexual involvement, then what one is proposing is no longer a *marriage* system. So, in the end, the proposal is actually incoherent: either the classification it proposes is

[18] Goodridge 11.

arbitrary and unjust (and so unstable), or it collapses into a proposal to abolish marriage rather than to redefine it. Providing certain benefits to all stable households, precisely because of that stability, would not be unjust. But that would not be marriage (and the injustices involved in privatizing marriage already mentioned would obtain).

A second problem with the incoherence in the same-sex marriage proposal is this. If it does not lead to the state's complete withdrawal from regulating marriage, or before it does so, it will gravely *weaken* the institution of marriage – which will harm spouses, potential spouses, and children. According to the conjugal understanding of marriage, spouses are asked to form stable or committed relationships because of something larger than each individual – because marriage is a basic human good formed by spouses as complementary sexual persons and because the family (the fulfillment of marriage) depends on fidelity and sacrifice. But on the revisionist view of marriage, people are asked to form stable relationships – for the sake of stability. On the conjugal understanding of marriage, there is a rationale, a purpose, for the stability – or fidelity – of spouses. On the revisionist view, stability itself is posited as the rationale. But people in such relationships are apt to ask themselves at some point, why *should* this relationship have stability? Why can't that be dismissed as an unjustified imposition?

Same-sex marriage supporters often say that they desire the norms as well as the status of marriage for same-sex partners (though lately some have argued that to insist on those norms for same-sex "marriages" is a manifestation of the evil of "heteronormativity"). The problem is that once they redefine marriage in order to include same-sex unions, they have removed the point of those norms. And if marriage is redefined in this way, then it will be harder for *anyone* to understand the norms of marriage. If people do not understand the rationale of norms, they are far less likely to adhere to them. Hence redefining marriage in order to include same-sex partnerships will lead to an incoherent view of marriage and to greater instability in the institution of marriage.

The Law on Divorce

We have treated the debate about same-sex "marriage" in great detail because of its timeliness. Yet, equally important for having (at least to some degree) a healthy marriage culture is the law's stance on divorce. More than twenty years ago, Mary Ann Glendon wrote that marriage was being rapidly transformed from a legal relationship terminable only for serious cause to one terminable at will.[19] Both in the law and in the culture at large, that transformation seems now to be almost complete – though not, we contend, irreversible.[20] Most of the state divorce laws in the United States changed in the 1970s from divorce only for grave cause to no-fault divorce. Today, in all fifty states, the termination of a legal marriage requires neither a grave fault, nor the consent of both spouses, nor even a significant waiting period. One spouse need only claim that there are "irreconcilable differences" or that the marriage has "irretrievably broken down." The divorce can be unilateral. That is, one spouse can end a marriage against the wishes of the other and without proof of any wrongdoing on the part of the "unwilling" spouse. Indeed, divorce today is treated more like a summary ministerial procedure than an actual lawsuit. Of course, the upshot of these changes has been to make divorce easily available.

This legal revolution was itself a major – though not the sole – cause of the dramatic rise in the divorce rate in the United States. The divorce rate has nearly doubled since 1960 (though it has declined slightly in the least decade – in part owing to the rising average age of marriage). For couples marrying for the first time, the probability of divorce now falls between 40 and 50 percent.[21]

Several arguments were advanced in favor of this transformation. It was argued that court proceedings to determine guilt

---

[19] Mary Ann Glendon, *Abortion and Divorce in American Law* (Cambridge, MA: Harvard University Press, 1987), 63–81.

[20] For an account of the rapid movement of the states to no-fault systems, see Herbert Jacob, *Silent Revolution: The Transformation of Divorce Law in the United States* (Chicago: University of Chicago Press, 1988).

[21] Institute for American Values, *State of Our Unions: Marriage in America, 2011*, http://stateofourunions.org/2011/social_indicators.php#divorce.

provoked unnecessary acrimony and that they led to manufac-
turing of evidence, perjury, and disrespect for the law. It was also
argued that courts were already granting divorces irrespective of
fault and so the change to no-fault divorce would merely close
the gap between the law and reality. And (though advanced only
years after the change to no-fault divorce) it has been argued that
most marital breakdowns occurred through no one's fault, and
so it is futile either to require a trial to determine fault or to delay
dissolution of such "dead marriages."

However, each of these arguments rests on false presupposi-
tions, to which we now turn. The most popular argument was
that the fault-based system placed the divorcing spouses in an
extreme adversarial position – requiring at least one spouse to
gather evidence showing grave fault in the other – and so caused
or increased bitter acrimony. Writing in the early 1970s, two
advocates of no-fault divorce expressed this argument as follows:

Perhaps the most damaging result of a "fault"-based divorce procedure
is that it exacerbates the aggressive forces that may be already under-
mining the family. It dissipates family emotional and financial resources
at a time when they are most needed. The hatred, bitterness, and resent-
ment fed by a drawn-out divorce are likely to destroy the possibility of
reconciliation and distort the negotiations and proceedings designed to
resolve the very difficult and emotionally-freighted issue of finance and
child custody.[22]

However, this argument assumes that the acrimony between the
spouses outside the court is roughly the same in the two systems so that the admittedly greater conflict in court in the fault-
based system means a net increase of acrimony. But this does
not seem true. When the acrimony not directly associated with
court proceedings is taken into account, it is far from clear that
a no-fault system decreases acrimony all told. The finalization
of a divorce does not, unfortunately, end the discord between
the former spouses, since they usually must continue to negotiate
visitation times and other decisions regarding their children, and

[22] Goldstein and Gitter, as cited in Lynn D. Wardle, "No Fault Divorce and the
Divorce Conundrum," *Brigham Young University Law Review* 79 (1991):
92.

the discord that was aired formerly in judicial divorce proceedings often shows up again during these negotiations. However, in a no-fault system, the bitterness here is confounded: a spouse who does not wish to divorce but wants custody of the children – usually the wife – has much less bargaining leverage under the no-fault system than under the previous one, and so she is often pressured to settle for much less in property division and support in return for child custody.

As Maggie Gallagher noted, discussing a study by Constance Ahrons (who herself tended to be overly optimistic about divorce),

Ahrons' study confirms what common sense suggests: Divorce is typically marked by much conflict, and the acrimony endures for many years. She constructs a typology of parents' post-divorce relations. It is not a pretty picture. In 50 percent of middle-class divorces, she found, parents engage in bitter, open conflict, becoming what she calls "angry associates" or, even worse, "fiery foes."[23]

Another reason there is continued conflict between divorced spouses is that many divorces in the no-fault system of today are unilateral: enacted against an unwilling, innocent spouse (innocent at least of traditional legal grounds for divorce). Such divorces often leave the unwillingly divorced spouse feeling abandoned and embittered. Indeed, marriage involves a close intertwining of the spouses' lives – emotionally, financially, and in many other ways. It has become clear that the goal of (equitably) dividing what was so intricately bound together can seldom be achieved without rancor, emotional harm, and injustice.[24] The economic injustice should not be ignored: for the spouse who retains custody of the children (usually the mother), divorce is often an economic disaster, whereas the other spouse's standard of living may significantly rise.

---

[23] Maggie Gallagher, *The Abolition of Marriage* (Washington, DC: Regnery, 1996), 103.

[24] For elaboration on this point, see Diane Medved, *The Case against Divorce* (New York: D. I. Fine, 1990).

The argument that no-fault divorce decreases spousal acrimony also assumes that there will be the same number of divorces in the two systems. Yet easy access to divorce sends the message that marriage is not a valuable enough union to protect by law, with the result that some spouses take their duties to their marriage less seriously than they otherwise would. In the last decade, there has been abundant sociological data indicating that no-fault divorce did indeed lead to an increased number of divorces.[25]

Furthermore, since it is likely that there are more divorces in a no-fault system than in a fault-based (or mixed) system, many families could perhaps have been spared the inevitable acrimony of divorce as well as the numerous other grave harms wrought by divorce. Their injuries are the price being paid for a lower level of acrimony during the divorce trial.

Moreover, the no-fault divorce system is itself unjust. By design, it fails to address the profound injustices perpetrated by one spouse when he or she gravely damages (or destroys) a marriage. It also conveys a false idea of what marriage is and the gravity of the real moral obligations one has when one marries. So it is likely that when one takes account of the bitterness in the whole process of divorce, as opposed to considering only the bitterness during the trial, there is as much or more acrimony in a no-fault system as there is in a fault system. But even if there *were* less acrimony (in a no-fault system), the price paid for that would be a larger number of divorces, grave injustice to many abandoned spouses (and to children), and a significant misrepresentation of the nature of marriage and its obligations in justice.

When a marriage breaks down, at least one of the parties (and perhaps both) failed at least at some level to fulfill his or her marital commitment. In many cases one party simply abandons the other and his family in the quest for a younger mate, or to "find" himself. To ignore and facilitate such grave injustice, in

---

[25] John Couch, "An Introduction to Divorce Reform and Other Marriage Issues," http://www.divorcereform.org/mmo.html.

order to avoid the acrimony of a trial, is a dereliction of the state's duty – a central part of which is to enforce and regulate contracts (though marriage is more than merely a contract) and correct injustices resulting from violations.

The second argument for no-fault divorce was that the previous system often encouraged spouses seeking divorce to manufacture grounds for divorce and commit perjury as a means of obtaining it. This in turn generated disrespect for the law. As the National Conference of Commissioners on Uniform State Laws explained in its report recommending a new no-fault divorce set of statutes, "the traditional conception of divorce based on fault has been singled out particularly, both as an ineffective barrier to marriage dissolution which is regularly overcome by perjury, thus promoting disrespect for the law and its processes, and as an unfortunate device which adds to the bitterness and hostility of divorce proceedings."[26] It seems that spouses did frequently resort to perjury and that the law on divorce did in many circles come to be viewed as a mere formality. But the argument that this fact supports a change to a no-fault system presupposes a very low evaluation of marital union. If grave injustices have been done, then the fact that some people will perjure themselves during court proceedings about those offenses is not a strong argument against such proceedings.

Moreover, the willingness to commit perjury was at least in part due to an already existing disrespect for the law on divorce, stemming from the false opinion of many seeking divorce that they were *entitled* to it and that divorce was a wholly private act the state never has any business obstructing. Improving the divorce laws should be part of a more general effort to educate about the importance of marriage and the critical duties of spouses toward one another and toward their children.

The third argument was that the courts were already granting divorces based simply on grounds of irretrievable breakdown, the assignment of fault being a mere formality. So the new

---

[26] *Uniform Marriage and Divorce Act*, National Conference of Commissioners on Uniform State Laws, 1970, http://www.uniformdivorce.com/UMDA.pdf.

no-fault policy (it was argued) would merely close the gap between law and the actual practice of courts. The gap between the law and court practices was indeed a problem, but such a gap can be closed either by lowering the law or by raising court practice (or some combination of those). This problem could be significantly addressed by the courts taking seriously the importance of the stable nature of marriage and actually enforcing the laws rather than allowing the gap to emerge to begin with. Our argument is that both the law and court practices should address the grave injustices involved in marriage breakdowns, especially toward children, and send the right message (or at least not the wrong message) about the nature and importance of marriage.

Finally, a fourth argument was that it is unrealistic to think that in most marriage breakdowns, there is always fault, or, at least, that predominant fault could be determined. Goldstein and Gitter argued,

> But the breakdown of a marriage is seldom the "fault" of one of the partners. It results, rather, from a much more complex interaction between two, and frequently more than two, personalities. Even if "blameworthiness" were taken into account it is often impossible to tell who is the "guilty" party, for one cannot know what conduct, intangible and even unintended, on the part of the "innocent" party may have driven the "guilty" party to his "blameworthy" act.[27]

As the numerous scare quotes used by Goldstein and Gitter indicate, the authors do not really believe that in most marriage breakdowns, there actually is any fault, blameworthiness, or guilt. But even if there is guilt, they claim it is impossible to determine which spouse is the predominantly guilty party.

But to hold that marriages break down through no fault of the spouses presupposes a false view of what marriage is, in fact, a self-contradictory view. Marriage is a stable union of a man and a woman in body, heart, and mind. It is not a harmony of emotions or a mere likeness in personality or outlook – which are good things to have in a marriage but things over which

---

[27] Goldstein and Glitter, as cited in Wardle, "No Fault Divorce and the Divorce Conundrum," 79.

the spouses do not have direct control. On the view implicit in this argument, a pledge of undying commitment is at best hypocritical, for it is a pledge of what is not within one's powers. However, marriage is a commitment and a covenant to live with and for one's spouse, subject to limitations owing to one's own sickness or other external contingencies – in which case the other spouse's pledge remains, as the phrase "in sickness and in health" indicates – and to be faithful to him or her. It is not a commitment (or contract) always to have blissful feelings about one's spouse. The direct object of the marriage commitment (and what the marriage contract obligates one to) is something one *is able to do*. One is never morally bound to do what one is not able to, but the obligations entailed by marriage are consistent with that fact. Thus, if both spouses live up to their marital commitment (and contract) to the extent that sickness and external contingencies allow, then the marriage will not break down. If the marriage has broken down, then at least one of the spouses has not lived up to his or her commitment.

But perhaps the court is unable to determine fault; perhaps doing that, as Goldstein and Gitter claim, is impossible. Of course, there may be instances in which it is impossible to determine fault or cases in which there is roughly equal fault on both sides. And if that is so, and if the court can determine that, then it must find accordingly, as courts have done for such cases in the past. Goldstein and Gitter claim that by the nature of the case this will almost always be so: "It is often impossible to tell who is the 'guilty' party, for one cannot know what conduct, intangible and even unintended, on the part of the 'innocent' party may have driven the 'guilty' party to his 'blameworthy' act."[28] But this implicitly views marriage (again) as in essence a mere harmony of feelings or personality. If, on the contrary, the core of marriage is a commitment to live with and for one's spouse, and forswear other possible romantic partners, then things that are intangible or unintended will not count as grounds for fault in civil divorce. Actions that would count as grounds for civil

[28] Ibid.

divorce will not be impossible to determine. We conclude that the arguments for no-fault divorce are not sound. We turn now to reasons for a change from a no-fault system to a different approach.

There are several reasons why the law should give greater protection for, and so greater enforcement of, the marriage commitment. First, providing virtually no enforcement to the marriage contract – that is, providing easy access to quick divorce – has increased the number of divorces and thus gravely harmed spouses. One result of easy and rapid divorce is that spouses frequently marry with an expectation that there is a good chance it will not work out. This low expectation often becomes a self-fulfilling prophecy because it leads to less investment of effort and commitment in general. By contrast, where marriage is valued more highly, spouses have and retain the attitude that marriage is a durable reality; they expect it to be difficult at times, but they regard it as well worth whole-hearted effort and patience.

As we showed previously, marriage is an intelligible good, a distinctive way in which men and women are fulfilled. When they marry, the spouses become united with respect to their whole lives, not just with respect to actions and resources of some part of their lives. Hence, in marriage, each becomes internally modified by this union; each spouse's life becomes intertwined with – an intrinsic and not merely extrinsic part of – the other's. So divorce cannot help but be a severe trauma, comparable to the amputation of a bodily organ. It is a wound from which – as survey after survey has shown – it is difficult to recover and from which some people never fully recover at all.

The idea that divorce merely permits the spouses to undo what they unwisely began is illusory: the link to the other spouse – especially (though not exclusively) when the marriage has borne children – will continue in many concrete ways. The divorcee's view of love and trust cannot help but be harmed. Moreover, there is solid evidence that many couples would have been able to mend their marriages if they had persisted. For example, in a large survey conducted in the late 1990s, more than three out of five couples in unhappy marriages who decided to stick it out found, five years later, that their marriages were now happy (either "very happy" or even "quite happy").[29] As John Couch, head of Americans for Divorce Reform, observes, "Therapists and marriage counselors have come forward to say that most marriages do not simply 'fail' because of fate or predestination. Rather, what usually happens is that people give up on their marriages because they're not as committed to making them work as they could be, and because no one has taught them the skills that people need to deal with the disagreements and disappointments of married life together."[30] Making divorce more difficult to obtain would send the message that marriage is in fact a momentous decision and entails strong responsibilities. And this change would actually save many marriages – a significant benefit both for spouses and for children.

Easy and unilateral divorce is unjust to many spouses. In most states, some form of unilateral divorce is available, and so one spouse can obtain a divorce against the will, and without the consent, of the other, and with only a short waiting period (if there is one at all). However, being and remaining married is plainly an important benefit to many spouses who are nonetheless abandoned. And so the deprivation of that benefit is a grave harm. The present divorce laws facilitate these injustices rather than protecting against them. Moreover, because it is generally known that divorce can be easily obtained, a spouse who wants to save his or her marriage has little bargaining power for reaching a just (or less unjust) settlement.[31] (In fact, spouses who want custody of their children often feel compelled to consent to an unfavorable financial settlement in return for an agreement by the departing spouse – who in many cases can more easily afford protracted legal disputes – that the departing spouse will not press for child custody.)

[29] Linda Waite and Maggie Gallagher, *The Case for Marriage: Why Married People Are Happier, Healthier, and Better Off Financially* (New York: Doubleday, 2000), 148.
[30] Couch, "An Introduction to Divorce Reform and Other Marriage Issues," note 19.
[31] Gallagher, *Abolition of Marriage*, Chapter 11; Glendon, *Abortion and Divorce in American Law*, Chapter 2.

Easy divorce sends the message that marriage and being faithful to one's marital commitment are often less important than personal freedom. Indeed, the law provides less protection for the marriage commitment than it does for business contracts. Thus the law fuels the general perception that the marriage bond, in itself, is quite low on the scale of what has value. One result is that spouses themselves – insofar as they are influenced by the culture – also tend to value the marriage relationship less and so invest less devotion, resources, and energy to enhancing, protecting, or fighting for their marriage. However, marriage (as we argued in Chapter 3) is a distinctive, intrinsic good that – like other intrinsic goods – requires effort, patience, and devotion.

Easy divorce also profoundly harms children. Although the ease of obtaining a divorce is not the only cause of the dramatic rise in the divorce rate from the early 1960s to the present, it has significantly contributed to that increase. But it is now clear, and confirmed by several studies, that children growing up in single-parent homes, or in homes with stepparents, generally have more negative outcomes than children growing up in intact families.[32] For example, children in such families are two or three times more likely than children in intact families to experience abuse, depression, school failure, and delinquency.[33] Marriage has been made to seem less important, less attractive, and less secure than it was previously, and so a larger number of men and women are opting out of marriage entirely, opting merely to cohabit instead. The rate of breakup of cohabitors is even higher (much higher) than that of married couples. So, the devaluation of marriage has led to a dramatic increase in the number of children living in

---

[32] High-conflict families also have a negative impact on children, but spouses that might be tempted to divorce and then choose not to are not necessarily destined to fight or to continue to fight.

[33] See Chapter 3, section 9, and note 8 in that chapter. Also see Mary Parke, *Are Married Parents Really Better for Children?* (Washington, DC: Center for Law and Social Policy, 2003); W. Bradford Wilcox, William J. Doherty, Helen Fisher, William A. Galston, Norval D. Glenn, John Gottman, Robert Lerman, Annnette Mahoney, Barbara Markey, Howard J. Markman, Steven Nock, David Popenoe, Gloria G. Rodriguez, Scott M. Stanley, Linda J. Waite, and Judith Wallerstein, *Why Marriage Matters: Twenty-Six Conclusions from the Social Sciences* (New York: Institute for American Values, 2005).

single-parent households and without the protection and nurturing of both mother and father.[34]

The present law conveys the message that marriage is, not a union of lives, with an objective structure and grave responsibilities, but an essentially emotional linkage, worthwhile only for as long as one believes it provides the emotional benefits one sought to "get out of it." The fact that marriage is a distinctive good, having an objective structure, and fully worth whole-hearted dedication and persistence is obscured. This makes it more difficult for men and women to participate intelligently and realistically in marriage.

Of course, reforming divorce laws will not by itself completely change the culture's misrepresentation of marriage. But because the law has significantly contributed to this mistaken view, it can contribute to correcting it. At the very least, the divorce laws could be changed so that they do not inflict injustice on innocent spouses and convey a radically false view of what marriage is.

There are various ways the divorce laws could be changed. A first step could be to require that divorces that are not founded on grave fault must be by mutual consent and after a waiting period – perhaps two years. (That way, many couples will no doubt determine that their marriage is salvageable after all and perhaps go on to have happy marriages.) Second, unilateral divorce should be only for grave cause, or at least should require a long waiting period, to discourage it.[35] And the grave causes should not include a vaguely described one, such as "unreasonable behavior" (one of the causes allowed in England and Wales, which in practice tends toward weakening the marriage bond).[36] The causes could include desertion (for a specified period), adultery, and actual or imminent threat of physical abuse. The essential

[34] Institute for American Values, *State of Our Unions.*
[35] In England the law still requires a five-year waiting period for divorce without consent.
[36] Thus, the reform of divorce laws could be modeled on the present law on divorce in England and Wales, with the tightening up of the loophole created by the category of "unreasonable behavior" as a ground for divorce.

point of changes should be to bring the law on divorce more into line with the real nature of marriage – a union of a man and a woman, in body, heart, and mind, not necessarily accompanied by blissful feelings – and with the important duties of spouses toward each other and toward their children.

Index

adultery, 70–71
affection and nonmarital sexual acts, 82
Ahrons, Constance, 130
Alito, Justice Samuel, 114, 119
Anderson, Ryan T., i, vii, 43
Anscombe, Elizabeth, 86
antimiscegenation laws, 120–122
Aquinas, 12, 23
Aristotle, 16, 17, 18, 20, 26, 27

basic human goods, 22–36
Bible, 15
Bigger, Nigel, 79
birth control pill, 2, 3, 4
Black, Rufus, 79
Blakeslee, Sandra, 63
Bogle, Kathleen, 4
Boyle, Joseph, vii, 23, 35
Bradley, Gerard, vii
Brown, Susan L., 107

casual sex, 3, 4, 21, 69, 95
Catholic teaching, 52, 65, 66
Chesterton, G. K., 63
cohabitation, 6, 67, 100
common good, 41, 47, 53, 56, 57, 67, 78, 80, 81, 82
consequentialism, 30–33

consummation of marriage, 47, 52, 60
contract, contractual relationship, 49, 52, 66, 103, 104, 111, 132, 134, 135, 137
Corvino, John, 91, 92, 93, 94, 95
Couch, John, 131, 136
coverture, 119
Creel, George, vii
Crittenden, Danielle, 3, 4

divorce, 6, 139
and children, 63
dualism, 5, 74

England, divorce laws in, 138
equal treatment, fairness, 98, 122
exclusivity of marriage, 61

fertility, 38
Feser, Edward, 16, 17, 18, 19
Finnis, John, vii, 12, 23, 33, 35, 71, 72, 92
fornication, 17, 77, 83
Fourteenth Amendment, 98, 122
friendship, 28, 41, 46, 49
function argument, 21

142 *Index*